The Human and the Divine

Testimonies of Restoration

Terry-Ann Grant

Fulton Books, Inc.
Meadville, PA

Published by Fulton Books 2020

ISBN 978-1-64952-376-1 (paperback)
ISBN 978-1-64952-377-8 (digital)

Printed in the United States of America

Preface

I have written this book because I believe it is one of many tasks that has laid upon my life as a purpose. Since being a single parent, I needed many skills to survive with my kids; as life expected me to tackle it with assurance and confidence, experience has shown me its ins and outs and also given me hope but not without issues. Many asked, "How do you feel?" and "Who is the giver of your strength?" I view as I shared the details of my supplier and what he has done, as I see where this has brought hope and needed strength to others.

Instantly I decided to share my life testament, not only to individuals but to all. Bringing remembrance to God, who never fails to offer life, favor, and grace, as we are all obliged to lean upon him. I have shared my thoughts, experiences, and victories throughout this book, hoping these words would regain faith and offer inspiration to others. I have forever lived by laws and examples of life, and one such law is observation; it has stood as a tool of guidance within my life.

The Human and the Divine offers inspirational poems of restoration and quotes given through visions and spiritual experiences, which we can all relate to in times of doubts, fears, and desires, supported with beliefs and evidence that provide balance and truth. My first idea of this book was that I was given the task to write a book of inspirational poems. Still, as I was writing, the Spirit of God offers thoughts to turn these poems into quotes and testament that offers issues that affect us as humans.

All these quotes have affirmed my personal experiences on an affair with family, tolerance, optimism, humaneness, and union, no intention or indication to offend anyone. I have completed my duty with no motive of gaining recognition, but only to remind humanity of its value, purpose, strength, and most of all, its Creator. I have no objection toward any organization, beliefs, religion, or any choices made by individuals.

My only goal is to share options of direction when one stands at a crossroads and to highlight the full proof of love within humanity. I have observed that individuals allow hate and corruption to direct their path without accepting accountability, and some denounce the existence of God simply because he is unseen. My desire and hope for this book is to remind humanity of its importance, expectations, demands, devotion, and humaneness, which should use as a strategy toward life given to us by God.

My pain and dismay, which I have shared, may come at different times, with different actions, and bring different effects, but it all brings a similar result of brokenness. Our situations may be different, but the strategy of self-assurance and self-worth will bring you happiness, life, success, and value.

I would love for humanity to take a moment to observe where we are coming from and look closely at where we are heading. God has given us willpower. A sense we should use to make our own decision, so I will never go against anyone's belief, as this constructs the foundation on which one stands, as your choices become the resource of your life.

I believe that we should be Christlike with our thoughts and actions and see creation as to how God sees it, by using his truth as a foundation of which we should stand on. I will continue to pray and do my part as an individual, to define the love of this world and its creator, who is God. I will never cease to show compassion to my fellow brothers and sisters, and I salute the brave men and women of this world who strive to maintain peace, love, and unity among humanity.

By Loving God, You Accept Humanity

꧁ ꧂

Put on therefore, as the elect of God, holy and
beloved, bowels of mercies, kindness, humbleness
of mind, meekness, longsuffering. Forbearing one
another, and forgiving one another, if any man
has a quarrel against any: even as Christ forgave
you, so also do ye. And above all these things put
on charity, which is the bond of perfectness.
—Colossians 3:12–14

As a child, I could not understand the reaction of those around me
because from those I should have seen as role models often reminded
me, I am an outsider. Children live what they learn, and in time, it
becomes a daily routine to excuse me from the midst of their togetherness as for that, I grew within isolation. Many say that isolation
can create a hazardous motive. But the result comes from the present
mindset of which you possess while entering isolation, which creates
good or bad reasons.

I often struggled with my feelings because I felt life has given
me more than what I deserved. Within isolation, I have exercised
thoughts of why I am not seen as equal within my family. I often get
confused, and that would cause thoughts of loneliness and feelings of
rejection within my times of isolation.

As I get older, life experiences have shown me its differences and
what it has to offer. At times, it becomes unbearable even to keep a
smile on my face. Growing up, the first feeling of fear, resentment,
and guilt I experienced was within my home and around my family,

5

which has given me the understanding we all created with differences of interests, likeness, and personality.

I have my first experience of fear with physical and verbal abuse under the disguise of discipline. And as I knew the story of my existence, the pain my mother went through, I felt guilty as I am the result of her misfortune. There were times in my life I would like to forget, but instead, I hold on to the memories to inspire or to remind myself of the things that make me who I am today and the ones I have not known, of which God as defeated on my behalf. I also reflect on the moments I do cherish, where my mother would share stories that bring us to laughter.

I accepted God within my life and in my isolation to receive answers. Did I receive answers to all my questions? I did not. But what I do get is that once you accept him to intervene, the Spirit of God creates oneness with you. I created a personal relationship with God, and by doing so, I found peace within my family no matter the differences that existed among us. I put my trust in God's hands because I sought guidance from him.

I have given thought to understand that humanity comes with diversity, not with divisions. God had created us of our image but also in his likeness. By that effort, we should all learn to accept the differences among us. We may be born within a sinful world, not by hate, hate taught to us by the actions of those either in our home or around our surroundings.

As a human, we celebrate events within our doings, mostly ones that bring joy to us. But with the reality of life, we can never hide from those events that bring us grief. Many we have lost, and often we ask God why. We seek to receive an answer from him, but most likely, we are so blinded at times with our fears we never receive the answers he offers to us. God made us of his likeness, so we are a representation of who he is, to be used as an instrument for his purpose. But we will never understand his will or his doings.

Leaders are created among us, whom we take directions from, as we look up to these individuals of authority within society. But one has given leadership as a form of blessing, with the guidance of God's authority, so one should always lead on the grounds of equality and love, rather than deny others rights. As people, we should be influential among ourselves, following the development of the present and future generations. To be informative to others, creating ways to reduce ignorance and careless attitude amongst ourselves by using the gift of understanding, as we continue to be our brother's and sister's keeper.

By knowing how to recognize pain, guilt, and confusion, we could offer good advice to restore unity among us. Having the right to pass judgment is not only to cast out or to place mentally or physically in any form of imprisonment. Instead, we should use our authority to create rehabilitation for those reclaiming their position within society.

We should willingly show compassion for those who need refuge as they reconstruct their nation after times of demolition. We should live with no regrets or remorse; continually, we should secure our future generation, never allowing them to be intentionally exposed to hate or ever to be deprived of acceptance within society.

Humanity is God's wonder, a remarkable miracle that has given life to this world. I have known the importance of creation and understand the diversity within my family. I have learned to accept all experiences with forgiveness since I allow God within my heart, because no matter the indifferences among us, we are still created to be one.

Unleash Thy Strength to Shift Your Obstacles

Fear thou not; for I am with thee: be not dismayed; for I am thy God: I will strengthen thee; yea, I will help thee; yea, I will uphold thee with the right hand of my righteousness.

—Isaiah 41:10

Living without battles and obstacles is like running a race without competitors. To be a strong competitor of life, you would have to accept any form of hardship by seeing it as a challenge rather than obstacles. I fight daily with the mentality of rejection as I struggled with acceptance throughout my life because I was a child of a broken relationship.

My mother was my defense within my home but, at times, appears weak because of her position. She could never win any battle on my behalf; as a result, I silently wrestle with self-worth and loneliness, as I was often afflicted because I was an outside child. At one point in my life, I felt as though I am an intruder within my family, and I am sure that we all felt this way at times. As we attract these emotions onto ourselves, we also creating a barricade within our hearts resulting from the actions displayed from others.

Many have asked how I dealt with my battles with no signs of fear or surrendering. I learned to endure hardship with patience by allowing the presence of God to intervene within my heart and doings, and this brings me the confidence to fight. I refused to be overthrown or broken by dismay, betrayal, or rejection anymore. With perseverance, I never lose sight of my purpose and the promises from God. Whether I win or lose, it still creates a difference and self-assurance within me I have fulfilled my path, and my result will determine how I approached the others.

We all possess physical strength, but not all battles require human power. We should learn to rely on the power and promises of God in times of need because he is the giver of physical and spiritual strength. As I approached my trials with steps order by His will, I know the more influential the aggressor, the more I leaned on the teaching from God. "I can do all things through Christ, which strengtheneth me" (Philippians 4:13). The higher the affliction, I remind myself that my God would allow my body to be beating and torn but never promise death any reward. "The LORD is on my side; I will not fear: what can man do unto me?" (Psalm 118:6).

The more I have been victimized, the more I have reminded myself that my reward is not from man but only cometh from the Lord. "Humble yourself, therefore, under the mighty hand of God, that he may exalt you in due time" (1 Peter 5:6). And higher the barriers told me, "Ye are of God, little children, and have overcome them: because greater is he that is in you than he that is in the world" (1 John 4:4).

These are the pearls of wisdom I have demonstrated to go through my battles. Faith has also taken me along the way with facing my obstacles. Not by only speaking the words of hope but also by demonstrating a life of faith. As I affirm the resources of my strength, I overcome all obstacles and achieve greatness within my life. I also learned to accept excellent or lousy criticism by using their remarks as motivations as these are also a form of battles in which we all face. Whether they are from families, friends, or spouses, they should never determine the accomplishment of your task, dreams, or success.

As I leap over my barriers, so can you, but before you challenge what you know nothing of, you must first seek a source of defense and strength, which is God. Believe it or not, He is one call away. He who created us welcome his presence and challenge your barriers with love.

God Gave Mankind Willpower to Pursue Greatness

❦

> But seek ye first the kingdom of God and His
> righteousness, and all these things shall be added
> unto you.
>
> —Matthew 6:33

My journey was and still not an easy one. A few years ago, I had
struggled and had thoughts of giving up and accepting my present
situation, but I could not give consent to this condition. As I knew
that nothing is impossible with God, I ask Him to intercede on my
behalf, as I was in no frame of mind to make the right decisions. And
with that, I would have to enable willpower to achieve my desires.

Growing up, they never told me I couldn't achieve success, but
they always reminded me that the access of wishes could deny by the
belief of those around me, and because of such a reason, I was never
given a fair share along with my siblings. So I have learned to accept
rejection rather than seeing it as a reason to give up. I had to understand that life has the power to challenge us along the way, and my
greatest challenge then was acceptance within my household.

I subjected myself to the will of others and their determination
of my life. I allow their views of my position also to change the vision
of my destiny. But with time, I outgrew the opinions of others and
let my step ordered by the will of God. I denounced their terms of
afflictions and allowed the words of God to stand as an armor over
my life. And within the course of meditation, my mind no longer
holds thoughts of their limitation. If it is not but one gift God has
given us, it is willpower, a gift of choice that offers change along the

pathway of life, of which we could bring forth our dreams to reality, that will create fulfillment in our achievement.

Many individuals have gone through these experiences which they could relate to because for one to accomplish all without hindrance, the journey would be impossible. I have asked myself these questions as I openly declared my task because I knew that I am only human and have the capabilities to fail at some point, these questions where used as a form of readiness within my thoughts as I journey toward my desires.

Do I know how to utilize willpower? Am I committed to allowing desires to become purpose?

Do I have the self-discipline it takes to obey orders? And do I have enough self-control by not allowing others to alter my direction?

If we allow the presence of God to intervene within our hearts, we will make the right choices. That would order our steps toward our rightful purpose, and with Him, nothing will hinder us from pursuing greatness. Finally, apply faith alongside willpower, and it will allow us to achieve greatness with an abundance. Hypothetically, people say. The sky is the limit. But what my heart desires for, of which my eyes cannot see, is my limit.

For those of you that can relate to my experiences, I would love for you to take these suggestions of how you can create changes toward your destiny. First, applying change within yourself as this will manifest changes toward your future and purpose. However, changes come with commitment, and without obligation, the essence of willpower becomes impossible. I shall continue to fight with all my strength to receive what has bestowed upon my life as a child of God, knowing I am created with authority to live abundantly, and I do pray that you will do the same.

Even in Darkness, You Shall Stand Firm

Then spake Jesus again unto them, saying, I am the light of the world: he that followeth me shall not walk in darkness, but shall have the light of life.

—John 8:12

I was not a big fan for celebrating my birthdays because it was just another day for me. I could remember on my thirtieth birthday; I sat outside on my mother's steps and cried because I realize that I had not completed my goals for that year, and it has passed. My stepdad said that I was too hard on myself and I should take it easy. I could understand what he was saying, but all in my mind was to get my goals done within a specific time.

Fear had also contributed to my life when I had my children. Before then, I did not give too much concern about death or even the thought because of loneliness. But having a child gives me a sense of being wanted, responsible, and complete. So my fear was built from the thoughts of them losing me, and I would leave them behind without protection or stability.

Friday night, my fiancé called to see how my day was ending. We talked for a bit, then he reminded me that next Friday would be my birthday. He was so excited to spend that day with me. Even though he been celebrating from the first of the month, he had planned for us to see the mega-hit opening of *Black Panther* that Friday. Excitement filled me; this movie was opening on that day.

The first Marvel movie of all black heroes, but with no luck, tickets sold out.

We made other plans on what to do that weekend. Maybe dinner or see another movie, but I quickly objected to that, then he decided on having a little party of just us and the kids, so I agreed. This birthday was also a third-year celebration that God had given me another chance of life since 2013; for that I was grateful.

On the following day after work, I stopped by the store to get a few foodstuffs for the house. After this, I got one of those route cabs because it was a busy Friday night. A taxi came along. I signaled to the guy before me to get in, but he took one of my bags instead and said, "Ladies first." As I placed half of my body in the car, suddenly the driver drove off. I fell from the car with my bags with everything on the road. It happened so fast everyone was surprised by what just took place.

They asked if I was okay and to see how bad I was hurt. But I just got a small bruise on my knee. Right as the driver took off, the cops chased after him. Everyone said that must have been the reason he took off—maybe he did not have a license. As everyone was busy to help, a guy asked if I wanted to go to the hospital; I told him I would instead pay him to take me home. He said, "You sure about that." I said yes, he took my bags, and we headed for his car. As we drove off, I reflected on what happened; suddenly, I was distracted by the driver making sure I was okay. I was fine.

Thank God for his intervention and that I came out with just bruises on the lower part of my knee. Because it could have been worse, he looked at me and smiled as he expressed his love for God too. As we approached my house, I handed him the money, then he came out to help me with the bags. "I don't know you but am in love with the spirit that's on your life." I smiled and told him I thanked God for that too.

Everyone was happy with the result because it could have been worse—a life could have lost—and we give glory for that. It may not be the same experience I have, but these attacks we wrestle with throughout our days either at work, school, home, and even as we commute. These assaults are designed by the darkness that roamed this earth to kill and destroy, but by his grace, he will protect us through it daily.

As I reflect on my past, I'm glad that on the day I accepted the presence of God within my life, my children have chosen that path too, and I never regret their decision at their tender age, making their own choices. God's promise shall stand for us through the midst of the force of darkness because he's the ruler of all things. He's salvation and refuge when we need him, fighting our battles even when we have no sight or knowledge of them, and he's our source and giver for life. I wish that all could welcome God within their life and allow him to intervene. Thank God for the day I choose to live in this light.

The Unity in Worship Creates Prosperity

With all lowliness and meekness, with longsuffering, forbearing one another in love; endeavoring to keep the unity of the Spirit in the bond of peace. There is one body, and one Spirit, even as ye are called in one hope of your calling; one Lord, one faith, one baptism, One God and Father of all, who is above all, and through all, and in you all.

—Ephesians 4:2–6

When I was a teenager, my mother attended church, wanted to serve the Lord with all her heart, and at the same time, wanted to bring the whole family with her on this journey. She was invited by her friend to visit her place of worship but did not achieve the spiritual welcome she was expecting. One morning, she got up, explaining to her husband about a dream she had of a place of worship, which she believed was ordained for her to visit.

She had visited that worship place before, so she knew exactly where to go. By the next Sunday morning, dressed and ready, she took along my smallest sister and left me, my young brother and my older stepsister, at home, with strict instruction of what to do. It turned out to be her worship home. She became a part of the worship family and also a part of the choir. I could see the differences in her life and the growth where her spiritual life was concerned; I could see she was home.

But before completion and contentment, she would have to complete her mission by guiding the whole family to salvation. My smallest sister and brother were no trouble to follow up on because they were not at the age to rebel against anything she said. My step-dad told her each Sunday that as soon as the pastor could give her the winning lotto numbers, then he would be attending. My stepsister was a little reluctant at first, but she accepted and got baptized. Now I am the one she went to war with; it was not because I didn't see the purpose of doing it.

But I was reluctant of the fact that I was feeling forced to make that step. I refused to see it her way. I was just not ready. I did not feel any spiritual sense while attending; the only part that got me was the praise and worship. That was it for me. The rest was boring, and I was getting exhausted, just sitting there. I knew she wanted to lead us on the right path, and with my mind bullied by the means she used, eventually with months of annoyance and side eyes, I was feeling guilty, but still, I refused to satisfy her need, arguing it was her place of worship, not mine.

I was more reserved than her. She was the type that attracted an audience wherever she went, so it was easy for her to feel at home. The fight went on for months after I finally surrendered to take heed of the lesson from Sunday school and the ones she added, and eventually, I agreed to give my life to God by accepting the ways and doing to a life of righteousness. Others may look down on the strategy she used to make sure her family unified in the house of the Lord.

And yes, at times, I agree with what others say, but time and experience adds changes within my thoughts. I saw what she was preparing us for—not having a worship family and not allowing the presence of God will let life seem like a roller-coaster of depression, fear, hardship, and confusion.

With unity in our society, either in our place of worship or home, it gives us the will to fight, to improve, to achieve, to be at peace in times of dismay. Even though I was not as active as my mother was in her fellowship, under the umbrella of their union with prayers, I was offered protection by prayers from that same fellowship.

They were times when conflicts arose; there were fights and issues none of us could deal with, but in the end, we all would come together by phone or visits, joining in prayers and worship, giving glory to God. I learn that whatever the steps, journey, or events are and whoever God uses to lead you in the light, what is most important is that you made a step. And by that step, you are covering yourself and your family in unity. With everlasting prayers hope will become present, and he will do the rest.

No matter where I would go, I could still hear her words of encouragement for us to have a union with a fellowship, one which taught the truth and to seek wisdom for ourselves. I continued to lean on the understanding and guidance of the Holy Spirit. She continued to instill the rules and requirements of worshipping in our home. Even though we all lived in our own home, neither did I make my mother's worship place mine; instead, I created oneness with God.

But many would rather have a bond of unity with God within a fellowship rather than a direct relationship, and I will never object to that decision. On the grounds that agreement among worshipers brings wholeness without segregated difference of religions. To have unity in our place of worship brings balance, knowing we are a part of a family. A family that shows concern and acceptance to all members, no matter the status they hold, we should always function as a representation of the body of Christ in one accord. Having unity in worship in our household creates a family with strength: one that can never be defeated. As it was said, "A family that prays together stays together."

Learn to Break Ancestral Curses

> Christ hath redeemed us from the curse of the
> law, being made a curse for us: for it is written,
> Cursed is every one that hangeth on a tree: That
> the blessing of Abraham might come on the
> Gentiles through Jesus Christ; that we might
> receive the promise of the Spirit through faith.
> —Galatians 3:13–14

Family curses are handed down from generation to generation
unknowingly by an initiator, an ancestral curse placed upon us
knowingly is the actions of family members. I will share a personal
experience about my son's father with you of what had happened to
allow us to understand that curse cycles come in different ways by the
choices we make.

It all started before my boyfriend and I decided to have a child.
We would discuss not allowing issues or anyone ever to depart us
from our child's life. We would never become our fathers. My boyfriend's issues with his dad allowed him to hate his father because
of what he had to endure without him being around. He always
said that if his father were there for him, he would have had a better
chance in life and he would not have suffered the hands of neglect
from his mother.

After a year together, we had a son; he was so happy. His conversation was all about preparing for his son; before meeting me, he
was living by the law of the jungle, a life which he knew so well. He
never thought of changing because the street taught him everything

18

he knew. He always said that meeting me was his new hope, a fresh start to a new beginning. Within the events of our life, he tried to be less involved with the activity of the gang. He never openly shared that side of life with me, and I had never met any members, and I was satisfied with those decisions.

After the birth of our son, his father took one look at him and fell in love. He never thought he would ever live to have a child; he made promise after promise to never leave his side. Before the time of my baby's delivery, he was on the verge of changing his path. He got a job and was working and earning from a nine-to-five job. He was at peace. He even attended my mother's place of worship and gave his life to God. We were planning on getting married, but within a few months of our child's arrival, he lost his job.

He was bent never to step back into the life he had known. Life became difficult, but our families contributed until either of us picked up a job. A few weeks later, I got employed, and life went on from there. One night I came home, and he was not around, and my son was by my mother's house. I went to get him, and she told me that his father had gotten a call; he had to rush out. She added that it looked urgent. I was not worried at first, but as time passed, there was this worrisome mood that suddenly came over me, but I thought little of it.

I went home with my son around midnight, after which I got a call, and it was him. He asked me if I was back, and I told him yes. He asked after his son. Then he said, "I was shot and am in the hospital."

The phone almost fell from my hands. "Where? Who shot you?" I asked, but he did not answer my questions. For an instant, I thought I was dreaming, but it was real.

He said that I should take care of his son. "Wait, don't say that—what happened?" I asked for a second time. I have never seen him again free; he had gotten a life sentence. All those promises that he made were broken. He unknowingly stepped in his own father's shoes. His father had chosen not to be in his life, but he was taken out of his son's life because of his chosen path in his past, a choice he had to take to survive.

I have seen and heard of many ancestral curses that have destroyed lives because we pass them off as bad luck. Another issue is when a child becomes rebellious toward their mothers. Many would say we should curse such children and separate your life from them, but we should remember that a mother's blessing is spoken words of prosperity for life, and a mother's condemnation speaks words that bring forth stagnation and even death. *So as a mother, why should I, who brings forth a life, nurture this life, and then deprive it of forgiveness?* I asked.

Right at this moment, your family could be experiencing one or even many curses in their life without understanding the reasons for all their afflictions or know how to solve it. An ancient evil can skip a generation by one action by someone doing or saying something positive. There are ways we can break these curses by offering forgiveness and acceptance. Start today by accepting the apology from a mother that given up on you, take the excuse from the father that wasn't around, accept the apology from a grandmother with words of judgment, and accept the apology from the siblings that saw failure in your choices.

Never Allow Diversity to Stand as an Obstacle

> And the evening and the morning were the fifth day. And God said, Let the earth bring forth the living creature after his kind, cattle, and creeping thing, and beast of the earth after his kind: and it was so. And God said, Let us make man in our image, after our likeness: and let them have dominion over the fish of the sea, and over the fowl of the air, and over the cattle, and over all the earth, and over every creeping thing that creepeth upon the earth. So, God created man in his own image, in the image of God created he him: male and female created he them.
>
> —Genesis 1:23–27

Humanity was created with diversity but after God's likeness, not intended to create hate and barriers among us or to live each day in a world that uses their differences as a weapon to create an obstacle.

Growing up in Jamaica, I have never encountered racism of the color of one's skin because Jamaica's motto is, "Out of many, one people." So if one should visit and you are of a different race, the only recognition you will get is by your accent and language because we all identify as Jamaicans. But still, I have seen where the diversity of culture, religion, politics, region, and wealth has played a path of indifference among our people. From my experiences, I am being labeled and denied opportunity simply because of my area in which I lived.

I see the horrors of those who are being gunned down by their choice of votes, the ongoing battle between religions, and the hurt of those who are victimized because they embraced their culture and beliefs. Differences in cultures bring reverence. It is a celebration of a nation's oneness of its values. My culture is recognized by our music, hard work, and hospitality by others.

We are known as a musical nation, but one such music genre that stood out in our culture is reggae music, a gift of melodies that often attracts the ears of humanity globally, as it is strongly influenced by our traditional music coming together with the strings, its bass, and drum downbeat sounds that send messages of love, peace, and unity to all.

Each nation has its cultural strength that stands as their identity, separating them from the rest of humanity, in ways of uniqueness, never in forms of segregation. Never allow others to hurt you, to hinder you from being the person you are. Always give love to whomever, no matter their differences; embrace with open arms, mind, and thoughts toward your brothers and sisters despite the color, likeness, and culture, and by doing so, you be embracing the greatest gift to this world, and that's love.

In school, we were taught the Jamaica Anthem and Pledge. My favorite phrase of the anthem is, "Teach us true respect for all / Stir response to duty's call, strengthen us the weak to cherish / Give us vision lest we perish." And I will forever stand with all the words from our pledge: "Before God and all mankind, I pledge the love and loyalty of my heart, the wisdom, and courage of my mind, the strength and vigor of my body in the service of my fellow citizens.

"I promise to stand up for justice, brotherhood, and peace, to work diligently and creatively to think generously and honestly, so that Jamaica may, under God, increase in beauty, fellowship, and prosperity, and play her part in advancing the welfare of the whole human race."

But as I observed what is happened around us each day, it hurts to see people victimized only because of diversity. More upsetting is when watching the same race building walls of injustice within their midst rather than strengthening and protecting each other. Diversity should be celebrated for the difference that exists within our cultures, race, beliefs, and only to divide us by regions. Being humane should be the course of our journey, as we allow the fellowship to be our bond. I hate to see where families separated and friendships broken by barriers of segregation.

I believe to be seen by the color of my skin, either black, white, or brown, should be an admiration not of evaluation. The level I pursued should not be restricted of me simply because you are intimidated by my strength, my place of refuge should be of peace and love and growth not of hate, loneliness, fear, and segregation, because of my origin. Whom I love should be a choice of my heart without fearing the acceptance of others. I should bravely stand on a platform, sharing my thoughts on issues that affect my community without fear of being criticized and judged because of my gender or my disabilities but only to be seen as a human.

Obedience Offers Respect, as Idleness Displays Ignorance

Who will render to every man according to his deeds: To them who by patient continuance in well doing seek for glory and honor and immortality, eternal life.

—Romans 2:6_7

I have always respected my elders and the advice they give. There is a saying, "No matter how high you stand, you will never see what your elders see or knew." I would sit all day and listen to the wisdom and teaching by my elders, no matter who they are, because I always felt honored and filled with knowledge whenever I am within their presence. I have experienced their life through the stories, and some were sad and somewhere happy, and others are for the purpose and lessons why there are living today. For all that I have heard, I noticed one formal word that had repeated over again, and that was *respect*.

My grandmother often told me being lazy is not likely of a woman, and I should occupy my time with either a book or doing household chores. At times, I would be annoyed by her constant proverbs. Still, I dare not be rebellious. She was always a hardworking individual, and she always reminded me of her life as a child. She had never gotten the opportunity to attended school or even have time to play; she had been withdrawn from school by her mother's situation and kept home to take care of her younger siblings, despite her eagerness to learn.

She would never disobey the words of her mother's command; she left solely to give attention to her siblings and grandma, while her mother went out of town to do house jobs. She talks about how life was difficult for her because of what she had endured at her age. Her grandmother was not of much help because she was also a working woman and her health was not helpful to her either. When she caught me giving attitude, she would slap me. Letting me know that I was lucky enough to have someone to teach me everything that required of me — and also can attend school, rather than learning life on my own, without an education.

Regardless of my grandmother's hardship, she has grown up to be one of the hardest working women I ever see in my life, and I have grown to love and honor her for who she is. I also celebrate her life each day that God has given her, with no form of education, she fights her way through life with no regrets, holding the weight of her family with perseverance and strength from the Lord.

She has done well for herself and for others; at times, she wishes she could have done more for us, but we have shown her in many ways that we appreciate what she had done. The battles of raising her children alone with little support but still stood firm with her beliefs that God will provide. With her faith, she has been blessed abundantly to where she becomes a giver. She had used the gift of cookery to feed her families and to feed others.

My grandmother was labeled a great chef because of her early training, resulting from being the homemaker from a tender age. To survive, my grandmother had a cooking business in the local market. Knowing my grandmother, I bet she had given away more than she ever sells. Best of all, she is my grandma, always seen her life as a purpose to serve, and she has done that in more ways than one. For all the hard suffering she has been through, I never heard her complain about anything, rather than if you ever serve her cold food.

She is such a humble soul, one that fights life with no preparation, armor, or weapons. She had taken on whatever battle that has given to her with perseverance and obedience. She refuses to be ignorant. By allowing life lesson to educate her in whichever way it directed, she would stand firm and endure with grace. "Respect is what takes you through this world," she would say.

Unveil My Eyes to See This World

After that, he put his hands again upon his eyes,
and made him look up: and he was restored and
saw every man clearly.

—Mark 8:25

I have seen this world throughout my natural eyes, but I have yet to see it spiritually. With physical sight, you will only see and read on the surface of all things and actions, but with the insight of the spirit, your thoughts and view become more in depth.

My grandma taught me to be my brother's keeper and always to give a helping hand when it is ever needed. You can never predict the ways of life; today may be your day of wealth and happiness and someone else's pain and needs because no situation is ever permanent. Being humane should be the first commandment of humanity.

I have had the opportunity to travel for work, and this opportunity has given me the chance to indulge in different races. Some you may end up living with and some you may only work along with, but no matter the situation, we all become a family. Sometimes, I have met and lived with my fellow countrymen and other times granted the chance to live among other races, where I can learn and enjoy their cultures.

The experience has become quite an adventure because of differences of interest and mixed emotions under one roof. I can remember all the rules my grandma instilled in me, and one of those was "Learn to live with the devil, and you will live with anyone." A thought that comes to mind when there is an issue. I have seen where jealousy create obstacles between friends, in ways of being ruthless, greedy, and dishonest. Also, I see where people use their authority to punish without a cause, and spouse infidelity becomes their partner affliction.

It amazes me to see the wickedness of the world encourage humanity to be immoral rather than being more virtuous. I would rather see genuinely compassion shown more frequently because we created to be one, never designed to be a destructive weapon amongst ourselves.

As I travel, I have also seen people of different nations, working together for bettering one region. It is funny how the eyes only reveal the differences of another by one's skin, where the actual indifference lies within oneself. Among this union, the aim becomes the interest of one country's economy, each as his motives, achievement, and purposes, but rather than allowing self-interest, they created a union instead, gathering together from distance regions, working together for the upliftment of one area.

This unity brings hospitality, entertainment, and love in service to others, I believe individually as a person, each as his strength to shift his rock, but imagine as a union, we can eliminate a mountain that forms a barrier between us. For society to perform such activities, it has to depend on the unification of the people coming together with faith, guidance, and allowing the interceding of God's presence with our doings.

We all need aid and supportive individuals around us, whether it is our family, friends, spouse, or workforce. Being kind should be a constant act of duty toward humanity, rather than using it to achieve recognition and self-praise.

I solely depend on the Holy Spirit to unveil my spiritual eyes under the authority of God. To allow me to see the world with love other than seeing it for its immorality. And for us to know the oneness which we should be as the body of Christ, to live with the abundant love and promises of God.

Allow Your Spirit to Signify My Strength

❦

The LORD is my rock, and my fortress, and my deliverer; my God, my strength, in whom I will trust; my buckler, and the horn of my salvation, and my high tower.

—Psalm 18:2

As I wrote these words, my thoughts bring me back to my past afflictions and doings, the experience was like carrying loads up a steep hill, could not compare the weights because either is still a burden. I never made a change in my life the day I baptized because, on that day, I never solely make that decision on my own. I was a teenager then with thoughts of why my father did not want me and still trying to rephrase the story my mother told me about my existence and the ordeal that took place within that time.

With all that I was also growing up within a household, which seems it was against me at all times, I could never catch a favor from my stepdad. I hold no thought of vengeance against anyone, but I never allowed them to continue to hurt me either; at one point, I fought back physically, then they accused me of being a rebellious teenager. I used to hang out a lot on the road with my schoolmates, for the reason that I didn't want to go home, and second, that was the only time I have any fun because at home, I was never allowed hanging out with the kids in the community.

My activity other than house chores was attending church with my mother on Friday nights, tarrying for the Holy Spirit, which I did not seem to receive. I was kneeling on my knees, with another individual speaking a language in my ears, which I could never inter-pret, and meanwhile, I was having thoughts about why I was here. *I will never receive this Holy Spirit,* I thought it as bypassed me because everyone was on the floor rolling and screaming from one end of the church to the other, and with that sight, I preferred not to indulge because the reactions of the others didn't inspire me.

I did not doubt what my mother and others were saying about the love of God because it was recognizable from the changes within them. The ordeals my mother went through after which she still stood firm allowed me to see she depended on some other source for strength to endure it all; the testimony of others permits me to believe that God's promises never fail.

Time has passed, and my choices have allowed me to make my own decision to receive the Holy Spirit. At twenty-six, I was a single mother with two kids. I made choices I regret and still hope for a promising result for the ones that existed. I never realize the impor-tance of accepting God as my savior has a child. But as I was to the point of brokenness, I let all my burden flow out from my eyes in tears, which I rarely do, because I allow myself to see such action as weakness and defeat.

I let go and look back to where God has accepted me, the cove-nant of which he bestows upon me, the hand he stretches forth when I'm in need, and the forgiveness he offers in love toward me, even as I was a step ahead from his presence. I could not understand but only feel what my mother or others were testifying about. Now that life had shown me its ins and outs, I realize that one has to experience for oneself for one to offer wisdom.

By accepting the journey toward salvation, it puts you in a place of transformation and rebirth, transforming you with heightened spiritualism. Walking the road of salvation, you have accepted deliv-erance from depression, guilt, confusion, and worries by gaining a new life of belief, restoration, and favor. Many have quickly revealed an act of sin, but have you truthfully bestowed the same announce-ment on oneself? I forgive all who have done me wrong, and I have also released all burdens by accepting peace within my life, and I am glad I was pushed to make that first step toward salvation.

Allow yourself to make this decision and only confess your misdeeds to God, never to others, for they have no authority to bestow judgment on you but will openly request for leniency, as it is a duty of humanity. I have publicly declared my past has settled, and I have accepted a life with Christ, causing all things to have been made new within me. My life has been strengthened by the presence of the Holy Spirit. I will declare his truth to others with glorification onto his name, as I continue to rely upon him always.

Walk by Faith and Live by Grace

For I am not ashamed of the gospel of Christ: for it is the power of God unto salvation to everyone that believeth; to the Jew first, and also to the Greek. For therein is the righteousness of God revealed from faith to faith: as it is written, The just shall live by faith.
—Roman 1:16–17

I have known only one way to live, and that way is through faith. I believe if I can have confidence and giving praise to a God I cannot see, then why can I not do all things through his name and receive the blessings he promised me?

I can remember a time where I found myself and my kids homeless. I was renting, and my landlord asked us to leave because she was offered more money for the apartment I had. At this moment, I would have to put my pride aside and move back my kids with my mother and her family until I got an apartment. It did not take long for the inquiries of a flat. I had refused some offers because of the areas in which they were, and some I would be too far from my mother's because she watched my kids after school.

We went out on Sundays to see where our luck lay; each gate we passed, we would knock to see if there was anything available. The area was not far from where my mother was living. It was two communities away, comparing to some we had heard of. After a few hours of walking, we stopped to ask this man standing at the corner for any vacancy. He told us of one that was two streets up from where we were. As we approached the gate, the dogs were barking. A lady stepped from the house, asking how she could help us. I explained to her of my interest in an apartment, and lucky for me, she had one available.

She assisted us in, from the dogs she had, and we walked along the side of the main house, to the back where she had the apartment. It was a one-bedroom, with a small dining room, kitchen, bathroom, and a porch; it was beautiful until she told me the price per month without utilities. My check was not enough to cover this expense per month and am a single mom with kids. I would not consider it; as my mother saw the expression on my face, she pulled me aside.

"Remember, you're just staying with friends, and the kids with me," she said. With that and a few other issues she added, I complied with the argument. And I accepted to pay this rent; she agreed to give me the apartment with two months' rent. Honestly, I walked out that woman's house not knowing where I would get that amount on the deadline she had given me.

For the next few days, I worked overtime, praying and hoping that I would make this happen. As a week went by, I was almost at my deadline. I was still short of cash to make up the money. I didn't lose faith or try to give up; I put in extra hours and meanwhile was still thinking of ways I could hustle the balance. My thoughts went to my father's sister who was living overseas. My aunt always told me if I ever needed any assistance I should call her.

I never did until this moment. I prayed within my heart as I picked the phone, hoping that my call will not be in bad timing. As the phone rang, I took a deep breath, my aunt answered, and through God's favor, I was blessed with the remaining balance I needed to complete payment. I was so thankful to her, at the same time giving praises to God for his intervention.

My kids and I were so happy to be living together again. Months have passed, and often I have sat and wondered how I went through all those months on a twelve-thousand-dollar check with ten thousand for rent. The remaining balance had to split between taking care of the kids, day care fee, food, snacks, and traveling expenses. I can say only grace carried me through and the people that God has allowed to place his favor upon my kids and me.

Faith is the things we wish and hope for, but he also uses grace as a favor to grant every blessing we receive, even if we are sinners or saved by salvation. God is not a partial God; the grace of God will be your refuge. His words will be the light that will guide you to salvation, and his grace will be bestowed upon your life abundantly. I can say that life experiences have pushed me closer to him, as I depend on his words for comfort and assurance. Even though many of us do not believe in the concept of faith and what miracles it does manifest.

Refrain from Self-Pity— Love Is Boldness

Behold, what manner of love the Father hath bestowed upon us, that we should be called the sons of God: therefore the world knoweth us not, because it knew him not.

—1 John 3:1

Love sustains our beliefs and bring forth God's will and promises. It has given me enough memories to reflect upon when I am at the crossroad of my choices, success, disappointments, and praise. So when I am standing at the threshold of my path, I think about how far back God has taken me and the love and protection he offers at all cost that created boldness within me.

Sometimes, I live only by faith; this reminds me of one period where I had no job as a single mother of two and a ton of bills to pay. With faith, I had the desire to do all things, but I would have to use boldness to request them. However, I have gone on job interviews with no experience on the required position. In those interviews, I spoke with the authority of God and requested that I could complete the task and for them to allow me to prove my capability.

I begged to be given two weeks' probation for it to be shown. After that opportunity, I worked within that establishment for two years and was offered a promotion. Boldness is also achieved with confidence. The assurance heightens my confidence with God's intervention throughout my life. This assurance allows me to see myself without fear and guilt, only with self-worth and love, because experiences have shown me who I am.

Experiences have assured me within my wants, "Not that I speak in respect of want for I have learned, in whatsoever state I am, therewith to be content" (Philippians 4:11). Whether good or bad experience, I have always sought for the wisdom within my trials, the in-depth message offered whether I am in dismay, joy, peace, or in need. "I know both how to be abased, and I know how to abound: everywhere and in all things, I am instructed both to be full and to be hungry, both to abound and to suffer need" (Philippians 4:12).

The love of God has shown me that "I can do all things through Christ, which strengthened me" (Philippians 4:13). Understanding the power of your creator, his will and his doing, will allow you to know who you are, what is required of you, and to believe that nothing that stands against you will ever succeed, of which all this knowledge will create boldness.

Having pity is to show mercy to someone and to show compassion to them in need of misery, affliction, grief, repentance, and hardship by reconciling indifferences between them, among them, or of oneself, restoring a bond of hope, love, and peace. Self-pity creates self-denial, self-murder, and doubts within our desires and purpose which God has appointed onto our lives.

No matter what was going on in my life, I never felt sorry for myself, nor have I ever felt as though I am not worthy of love, purpose, or accomplishment. The reason is that I have learned that if it is not yours, it will never cross your path. I have endured a lot of experiences that would quickly lead me down a pathway of self-pity. Because I never thought of myself untouchable of any affliction, because I am human. My advice to you is to enrich your thoughts with God's promises and love, and this will offer peace and assurance in all that you do. Learn to be still and know that God is in control, and accept your worth as a child of God with boldness.

Failure Never Lingers on the Path of Perseverance

❧

If ye abide in me, and my words abide in you, ye shall ask what ye will, and it shall be done unto you.

—John 15:7

There are times in everyone's life when some elements defeat us, such as ambitions, relationships, achievements, and even our love for God. Challenging us with trials and afflictions in which our purpose becomes hopeless and fear becomes our companion. I admire my grandmother's eagerness toward life, no matter its ups and downs. She will make the impossible possible; even at her age, she still possesses the strength of an ox without complaining.

I have always tried to do my best in all my doing. I can remember attending school. My principal would let us repeat this motto each morning: "Only the best is good enough." Throughout my life, I have carried those words with me for assurance, that I would give life tasks my best. There were times I felt like giving up, but when I look at the faces of my children, it reminds me why I continue.

With the assurance knowing that the Lord will take us through it all, I can remember that day when reality opened my eyes to the fact of me being a single mother; my desires of having a family had just become unfortunate. But it was easy for me to adapt because of the experiences I have gained and the passion I developed from all the women in my family.

Even if they were married, they were still pioneers in their household, though I sometimes was sheltered from many afflictions, helped by my family. Sometimes, I would have to stand and carry my worries along with one child, plus being a single parent for the second time; I instantly felt disappointed with myself. I can remember dating my second child's father; he had made so many promises but with time, life reveals all truth even when it is a lie. Soon, as I was six months pregnant, I was a single mother again, along with my son, at age four.

I became confused, wondering to myself, *Where did I go wrong?* People may say you should not have let this happen twice. But what if someone came in your life saying all the right words, doing all the right things, and most importantly, being a father to your child—you see your child looks at him with admiration. I asked, "What would you do?" I have played out scenes in my head of conversations and promises we made to each other, but I guess the only ones that manifested were mine.

I accepted my fate and instantly took on the role of being the mother and father to my children. With help from family members such as my aunts, mother, grandmother, and uncle, who is now deceased, all played their parts, allowing my burden to be reduced. As time went by, life became harder for me, even though I was given a helping hand, with the little savings I had. This carried me far with paying rent and other bills till I gave birth to my daughter.

Three weeks after giving birth to my daughter, I took a night job at a bakery from 8:00 p.m. till 6:00 a.m. Each night, I would pack my kids up and take them to my mother, then pick them up in the morning, go home, get my son ready, and walk him to school with my daughter. As soon as I got back with her, I tried to do all my chores in the house before returning for him at school. Getting back home, I would feed both and then try to get some sleep before work time. It seems puzzling how I endured all this. *Where does my strength come from?* I asked.

I can honestly say, looking back, I have taken nothing for granted. And I have never taken one step backward. It was hard, I can tell you. It was not easy, and it still is not. Throughout all my trials and dismay, on every side, I promised myself never to be distressed, knowing that my Lord would never forsake me.

I have been comforted and provided for by God; God always makes the impossible possible, just as he did for my grandmother, alongside our hard work and determination. I had my kids pushing me, but even if I did not, I have always dreamed of being someone important, with some credentials in this world. Advice to you as you continue to abide by the words of God within your life: never cease to push yourself to the limit, and God will do the rest.

I have not yet reached my goal in life, but I can say I am on my path of getting there. I decided never to fail. I will encourage you to do the same. I fight a good fight with the Lord by my side. Accept his presence, and allow him to be in your midst; with his blessings and protection and your perseverance, there will only be victories.

Every Battle Needs Compromise and Defeat

Be strong and of a good courage, fear not, nor be afraid of them: for the LORD thy God, he it is that doth go with thee; he will not fail thee, nor forsake thee.

—Deuteronomy 31:6

"The race is not for the swift, but for the one that endured it." Winning is not always being victorious. To be defeated can do or save us a great deal sometimes, with success, desires, arguments, relationships, and even with death, but at times we walk with death without a fight. Except for honorable men and women of our countries who committed their lives, defending us from those who threaten affairs and safety of humanity.

Even in our daily struggles with life, some of us have fought while others gave up; I can tell you it is hard to stand with confidence, facing life and the weight of its burden as your journey continues. We can never escape responsibilities and battles—why? Because the same determination which we use to achieve our desires will bring forth its fruit in time.

The other fights we wrestle with is life and death. To solve this battle is to accept that where there is life, death can be present. I understand that no one wants to die. But we also stop living as soon as we see things not going our way. We all fail at some point, and many say we are weak. I will be unfair to say that it's easy, because no matter how brave you think you are, no matter the wealth you possess, life will teach you lessons you wish not to learn. So humbleness may seem like a defeat, but I see it as grace.

As parents, most battles we fight are with our children. We teach our children right and wrong, we offer them the best education, we provide for them, we protect them, and we also fight for them. By doing these things, we are showing them love and training them to become respectful men and women of this nation. But as parents, we must compromise when these men and women chose to live their life by their own choices, as they are going off the course we set for them.

We can only pray they make the right choices, pray for their protection, and love them no matter their downfall, as these are our only responsibilities when they become adults. To either be defeated or to compromise all depends on the confidence, love, and self-worth you have given yourself. Sometimes losing a battle earns you more value than winning; the secret is knowing when to be defeated and when to win.

I have always chosen to put my troubles in God's hands through prayers, allowing him to direct my path and knowing the grace of God affirms my victory. We all are human, and we only see this world for what it is, yet ignorantly, we do not know the depths of its doing. Keep focus, be kind, and allow time to foretell its future.

Your Purpose Is to Suppress Fearfulness

Have not I commanded thee? Be strong and of
a good courage; be not afraid, neither be thou
dismayed: for the LORD, thy God is with thee
whithersoever thou goest.

—Joshua 1:9

"What's my purpose in this life?" I asked.

Some may have figured it out by now, while many are still searching. Others have stood face to face with their purpose but are still wrestling with procrastination, and a few have no clue. Fear and procrastination are related, I swear! Because these are the main challenges to overcome when you're trying to achieve anything in life. After all, if you do not fear issues, you're waiting for sign or time to make your first step, and without overcoming those hurdles, you will never succeed.

Often, people say I come off fearless to them. Still, they will never understand that I am so fearful of everything I do. But I will never allow it to suppress me nor my purpose. Even with the composing of this book, I was worried about how readers would view it and what their thoughts would be. Procrastination was my fight. I would instead think of something else to do rather than writing, even when I overcame it and got to work. A few words in, I would be distracted by a phone call or other events that would arise within a moment of my task.

For one to show obedience in being used by the Spirit of God comes with stability. I accepted to be guided by the spirit as I placed my profound thoughts within this book. I hope these words will bring hope, peace, and love, allowing you to know there is still hope in humanity with God, and that pushes me forward.

Our purpose brings not only success but also tests. However, I try to go through these tests without fear because I see them as a form of signals that assure me I am on the right path. Your mission defines your character, so try to stand firm with faith. The devotion you have shown, passion, and determination, toward achieving your goal, will suppress all your fears.

Humanity itself tries to be humane, given the gift of life to maintain the purpose and cycle of life. A few of us were blessed with the capability to lead, while many pursue it; others were given the knowledge to create. Many learn the ways of preserving it, and we were all given the authority to be knowledgeable, profitable, and fearless.

To suppress your fears, you would have to surrender yourself to your mission. Knowing your pathway designed by your creator and by accepting the path, you also recognize that it will not be painless, or smooth, and sometimes, you think that you're not worthy of the task. But by surrendering to your purpose, you are also surrendering to God, allowing him to intervene as you strive for success.

Encourage yourself by heightening your belief toward your journey, despite all the encounters of afflictions. Use your purpose to destroy every sign of negativity. And use your aim has a weapon against fear, pushing past all the elements that signified distress on your path. Remind yourself of where you are coming from and what it takes to start this journey. And you can unleash yourself from all the fear that's preventing you from succeeding. I'm encouraging you to hold fast on your belief. Whatever your course may be, you will pursue it with grace, and so will I.

"If ye abide in me, and my words abide in you, ye shall ask what ye will, and it shall be done unto you" (John 15:7).

Eventually, My Impossibilities Become Possible

And he said, The things which are impossible with men are possible with God.

—Luke 18:27

If I embark on a journey on which I have no idea what promises it has in store for me, then I will be only relying on faith and time to see the *possibilities*. Dreaming of the possibilities is easy, but for you to know the reality of its promises, you would have to make the first step; without that step, you can never identify its potentials. It wouldn't be easy, but I can tell you it will be worthwhile.

I can remember a time in my life I was broken and confused, not knowing which direction to go with the desires within, which could bring changes within my present and for the future. Being a single mother put me in a position to play both roles of mother and father; at first, I thought it would be *impossible* for me to tackle both tasks. Some opportunities that surrounded me didn't seem suitable for either my kids or me. I felt as if I was not enabled to make these desires *possible*.

Mentally and physically, I felt as though I had failed my kids. I had always stood against ever leaving them, but with no other choice, I would have had to settle with going away for the effort to make a change. It would be *possible* that my mother would take them in, but I thought to myself, *Would it be a possibility that I'm making the right decision to work a thousand miles away?*

Sometimes, your results are not what we had in mind, but remember, the journey was all about the *possibilities*. Every choice I make is always for the betterment of my kids, without knowing if it would be an inheritance to them. I have always put my kid's interest before mine, which I do so often. It needed a sacrifice, and each time, my desires stand in the form of those sacrifices. Being away from them, I have been homeless twice.

This journey allowed my kids to gain a higher level of education and their needs filled. This also brings blessings to those that were around them because of God's gift of abundance. With the sacrifice I made being homeless, on the third night, he opened a door of opportunity from a friend. She was talking about her friend requesting for live-in help, and the duties were only to do small chores. She even added that the individual could still be able to hold another job. I instantly accepted the offer. It was a blessing within the midst of time; I was so grateful to her for the offer and information.

Whether failures or rewards, I have embarked on journeys in my life based only on faith, hoping that I would achieve something either positive or negative. With no intention of denying that all could go wrong with a simple turn, still, my desire would become possible but not without battles. For every wish you have, there are always ways of achieving them; it's merely a task of seeking ways and taking steps for the opportunity to become *possible.*

As we journey on this pathway of life, despite the hardship, tears, pain, and dismay, there is always a *possibility* with changes, as no man's position is never permanent. With perseverance and commitment, all things can be *possible.* Sometimes, your desires are shattered, but it may be a *possibility* it is not destined for you.

Even our beliefs become a *possibility* to others and among worshippers because of other people's views and reasons that God does not exist. God is not a god of confusion, and with his presence, all things become *possible.* As children of God, we have the authority to know that all things are possible by his will. Even with the desires I had, a single step I have made by faith has brought change.

God is not a god of chance and possibility; the possibility is our humanly thought of hope to what we cannot see, but if we did all things with the conviction of faith in his will, all things would become *possible* to us. God is the purpose of my blessing because within this journey, he has ordered every step and allowed others to placed favor upon my life, while making the impossible possible with the *possibilities* which I seek to achieve.

Don't ever let anyone declare that your possibilities are impossible. With faith, commitment, hard work, and devotion, all things over time will become possible. First, have a personal relationship. Wrap up in the forever presence of the Holy Spirit. Life will become tenable and calm. Because the presence of God brings peace and promises, by embracing the love and acceptance that surround you, it will manifest your *impossible* to be *possible*.

You're an Instrument of God

But the LORD said unto him, Go thy way: for
he is a chosen vessel unto me, to bear my name
before the Gentiles, and kings, and the children
of Israel.

—Acts 9:15

If I were a real instrument, I would love to be a drum set. As my
drummer beats my bass, it would give beating sounds of hearts that
unite as one flow. As he taps on my cymbal, the tinkling sound would
be like chains falling, breaking free the diversity which sets us apart.
My snare drums would give sounds of liberation, and the sound of
my tom-toms would send a loud noise of unification. Unfortunately,
I am not a drum set but a human being, one of many created to be
an instrument of God's purpose.

Being approached with an opportunity to work in a spa, at first,
I was excited about the offer, then I realized that I would need to
leave my kids behind, but this opportunity would make a lot of difference in our life. I inquired about the contract, and it seemed I
would be away on this island more than being home. I would be
given only two weeks' vacation time with pay, but any other would
be my cost if granted.

I made some arrangements, and I went. It was beautiful and
peaceful, but I have learned, being away from your family and friends
becomes an adventure for the fittest. My first day at the spa was
great. Everyone greeted me, and I was now a part of a team. My living accommodations were excellent. I was staying at my employer's

house until I got my own. They were a husband-and-wife team, a very generous couple.

My stay would expire soon as the other employee arrived. Then we would get an apartment for both of us to share. My first week was great. I met a lot of clients, and I was up for the challenge of showing off my creative side, in the meantime demonstrating my professionalism to my employer. At home, I got on well with the rest of the family. My lady boss became my second mother, and her husband was the father figure I never had. A couple of weeks went by, and the other employee arrived.

She stayed at the house for a little while, and then we moved in together. She seemed quite easy to get along with, and the relationship blossomed to sisterhood. As time went by, her pretense faded and reality presented itself. My housemate acted shady, and she always kept me up-to-date with all the gossip they were having about me for reasons I couldn't figure out, but I still took heed of what she had to say.

In every gang, there is a leader, and she didn't like me. My housemate says that she hated me because of the relationship I had with our employers. "It seems you have taken her place," she said. Still, who's to believe what anyone says? One person can never hold a conversation; it's the effort of a whole team or two individuals. I thought the behavior was childish, with all this resentment toward someone you never tried to know.

But who was I to tell an adult she needed to leave childish behavior? This behavior went on for quite a while. At one point, it becomes so visible that my employers noticed and came to my defense. People fail to understand that when you try to beat on an individual without cause, they become a lamb before God. At one point, I felt like an outcast, but when I thought back on the purpose of why I was there, I put my attention on how I could earn more money to shorten my time.

Being a massage therapist was a golden job, and I never doubted myself on any challenge. So I sought around the island how I could get trained as a therapist; but there were no vocational schools on the island. My informant suggested that I take the book course online, then they would give me the hours in training that I needed to achieve my goals. I took the advice. I told my boss about my findings, and he was excited for me and also his earnings. I put my focus on what I was trying to achieve rather than trying to kiss up for friendships.

I got an apartment and lived on my own. I completed my course with honors, and all they could say when my employers were giving me congrats was to ask if my school was accredited; one even took it upon herself to check the school credibility. My employer then suggested that they would all chip in to help me to gain my hands-on score, as they were more experienced therapists, and they refused. By the grace of God, I achieved my hours from one of the reputable therapists on the island.

Rosa, I send you recognition for what you have done, to help make it possible for me, all the gratitude I received from my clients. I have gained the respect of being one of the best therapists around. I was determined to make every negative force my driving force to success in every way, and I appreciate my struggles because without them, I would never know my real strength and willpower.

I have gained so much progress from my battles. I have been an instrument of God's purpose. With obedience and with one accord, we all are instruments of God's will, which brings rhythms of peace and prosperity for all. So I challenge you today, be an instrument that brings promises, rather than musical notes of meddling, and even the height of the sky will never be of limitation.

Never Place Judgment on Your Past

Remember ye, not the former things, neither consider the things of old.

—Isaiah 43:18

"Your past is your past, and your present is your present." My grandmother would repeat such quotes to me as I murmured about my past. I'd get confused, because she would also say, "You should never forget the past" and "Never burn your bridges no matter your circumstance."

Often in our lives, we regret our actions, steps, desires, or choices we made in our past. Some may cause pain, while many have brought conflicts and confusion and even death, but how can we leave the past? How can we forgive and forget those events? People say, "What doesn't kill you make you stronger!" But how can we put all this anger aside or able to use it to a positive effect? No one knows your pain, and even as you try to allow them to see the perception of the pain, they will only understand.

How can I reclaim back my sanity to even love those that hurt me and to live again? Many of us still use our past as oxygen, and ignorantly, we also use it to denounce, restrain, and escape, doubting our privilege to give love, to accept love, to achieve, and to forgive. Despite the memory, we should still believe we have the authority to progress in every way, no matter our past.

Giving an excuse for our past can create limitations, as we use it as a defense approaching our present and future. We ask, "Can I overcome my fear from the result of being abused by a father?" Yes, you can, by allowing love to heal all wounds and allow forgiveness to reclaim your identity. "Can I be able to see loyalty, even though my mother abandoned me?" Yes, because loyalty is seen with time, and will be shown in ways of respect. "Should I refuse to be virtuous because of racism?" No, for your differences set you apart from others, and your uniqueness brings you value.

"Should I dismiss the purpose of living because of the hands of deceptions?" Never allow anyone to steal your joy because the Son of God was sent to us has our saver, knowing it would be achieved by deception. "I have created a barricade against being humane, how can I redeem myself from this imprisonment?" Wisdom brings freedom. So "Be not forgetful to entertain strangers: for thereby some have entertained angels unawares" (Hebrews 13:2). "Can I use the same willpower that I have used to build barriers to achieve independence?" Yes because "I can do all things through Christ which strengtheneth me" (Philippians 4:13).

I advise you that completing a journey of a maze depends on the order of steps you must take. The first step is accepting God as your savior, knowing that all things become possible. Once you agree with God, you become a new person in Christ, as you understand the steps to redeem your sanity with happiness, humor, acceptance, worth, courage, and forgiveness.

These acts should stand as a symbol of strength, which will elevate your passion for living, and never allow your past to become a weapon or excuse within your present. By placing God at the forefront, he will stand as your beginning and your end, and by these steps, he will never allow you to fail.

Learn to Control Your Anger

> Let no corrupt communication proceed out of your mouth, but that which is good to the use of edifying, that it may minister grace unto the hearers.
>
> —Ephesians 4:29

"Words is wind; action is the thing." Childhood memories. In my junior years in school, before a fight would break out, there would be a battle of words exchange between the two rivals; there were insults thrown on each side until the bravest throws the first fist. As we grow, we intend to forget childish things. One slogan of humanity is "free speech." However, does free speech give you the right to construct segregation, hate, abuse, blasphemy, and partiality within humanity?

I can remember when I just came to this country and I was trying to find my place in this vast political side of the world. I have learned the history of the indifference amongst humanity in a short period, which I have never experience firsthand before. It was the time of political change, and everyone had made a vote, along with backlashes of opinions. Honestly, it was an ugly sight to see humanity allowed the view of the minority, to bring changes to our effort and achievement of which our ancestors have died for us to achieve; instead, we should continue breaking the barriers of division amongst ourselves.

I wonder why we allow them to satisfy their egotistical desires, revealing their unseen hate and insults to those that strive against discrimination, partiality, and wars. Many may disapprove of me, using the term *minority*. Still, many of us have moved past the history that has place racial segregation as a driving force to our future, so I will keep saying they are just mainly minorities. My working environment was just as diverse, being an individual that never placed indifference on another by race.

I have always treated everyone humanely no matter who they are, but I guess not everyone appreciates it. Rather than showing gratitude, they offer you insults with words of discrimination. Honestly, I could say those words cut deep, but I composed myself, and instead of me retaliating, I answered her with words of reassurance, that we all should elevate our mind from the past invoked upon us by others. We are often pushed by others to be in a state of being mad.

I would say for myself if that day recalled a few years early. I would have reacted otherwise, knowing I am not strong enough dealing with temptation because of my uncontrolled temper. It was a long road, but I have developed the confidence and strength within me to create a shield of defense to deal with the situation at hand.

We are also human with limited supervision when emotions are overwhelmed by affliction, immorality, and verbal attacks. The infect of anger can destroy families, relationships, and characters. We should be able to suppress our temper when it becomes infected by rage. Learn to restrain your anger with modesty. I often heard that a soft answer turned away wrath. It's not impossible to achieve with the practice of diligence and by adding modest decisions to the next step you make.

But I ask, how can one take caution of what he or she delivers from their lips? Many intend to blame the tongue for revealing, but how can you when the tongue is only a messenger from the heart? I assume we should learn to reconstruct the emotions of our souls; above all, we lean on anger mainly as justification for the hate we speak upon others and upon ourselves. I trust my willpower to do all things, but can we be trusted to determine the direction of our feelings?

What we are failing to see is that words have the power of life and death. It can drive a nation to destroy each other. Words can cause hundreds of lives shattered, but with beliefs, words can also bring healing, prosperity, and peace. By controlling my anger, I humble myself before God and humanity; I have also learned to contain my wrath to a point where I offer a smile than fights. Even if you are being attacked, you can still arrest the profane, vulgar, verbal abuse from which as said. By feeding your thoughts with encouraging words of inspiration and elevating your feelings from dirt remarks, by replacing it with words of love and grace.

Your Character Is Like a Seed

For nothing is secret that shall not be made
manifest; neither anything hid, that shall not be
known and come abroad.

—Luke 8:17

Ever since I've known myself, I have tried to guide my reputation,
and for that, I've strived to gain oneness with the Holy Spirit for
guidance and understanding.

To be characterized is to be defined. Your personality is a per-
sonalized quality you have earned upon yourself; it will always stand
as an account of who you are. Some character is either obtained or
inherent, but the real work is how to sustain it by knowing who you
are and how important it is to live up to the rules expected. Which
will always be our battles, where the standard of one's character can
also be shown in times of hardship or success.

As early in my teen life, my friends have tested me because they
knew my afflictions. I am a fatherless child, so I have never enjoyed
the pleasure of advice and guidance from a father figure has others
do. In every area of my life, I was limited; I was told that all would
pass, but for now, I should figure it out. Sometimes I wonder what
age a person figures out his own life, choices, and responsibilities.

The feeling seems as if you take a child and place in the middle
of a jungle with wild animals, with no expectation of survival. Some
of whom that have known of my struggles have advised me to run
away from home. Others have offered me opportunities which would
bring me loads of money in a short period, and I could do whatever

I want. "No one will ever have the chance to hurt you again," they would say.

Even as a child, my level of thoughts was as deep has a pit, of which I spend most of my time within my mind. When given advice or suggestions, I would ask myself questions like why, if, and suppose, as I made my choices. I have seen a lot of character change in times of success within friendship, families, and between spouses, and often success allows one to be bold in his wickedness.

I believe that with hard work and God, we all can succeed. Some may achieve more than others, depending on the foundation led out either by parents, family members, and spouses. But with all cases, I believe we all should be our brother's keeper in any means to help those that are less fortunate.

I've learned to endure a lot through life experiences and never lived above my needs. But our choices are most affected by desires, not by needs, and our options become crucial to either uphold our character or either to sacrifice it.

Poverty is the most significant affliction that can either humble our personality or bring us to complete darkness. And often, poverty brings out the best aspect of survival ethics we didn't even know we have. It has its ways to redefine one's lives in ways you never expected, but it all depends on the directions in which your thoughts and motives flow. Negative thoughts will arise as disguised resources, appearing to be solutions to our immediate needs, and the reasons for us accepting these offers are caused by being blindsided by our needs and not of who we are.

Success has its ways of allowing one to reveal selfishness and ego, a quality that others didn't know you possess. Success is a great accomplishment, but one can become hardened by the struggles in which he endured to become successful. Others will be compassionate, helpful, and even moved to create resources for others to profit from, but it all depends on the motives of giving back.

Our beliefs have a significant effect on who we are. Through our ways of believing in God, we will find ourselves. In that way, we will believe in humanity, and our beliefs will allow us to act humanely toward others despite circumstances. By maintaining a good character, this creates a good reputation that should guide one's life, which will channel greater success to oneself and those around us that share the same perception that will give you the sense of obligation to live within your truth.

Forgiveness Brings Restoration and Peace

Instead of your shame, you will receive a double portion, and instead of disgrace, you will rejoice in your inheritance. And so you will inherit a double portion in your land, and everlasting joy will be yours.

—Isaiah 61:7

I could remember as a child, I have always felt as if I were alone in this world, and in times of trouble, it revealed that protection would never be offered without obligation in return. I was reminded that my presence in my family house was just for my mother. Every chance they got, it was their duty to inform me of the family name and its legacy and how it was not extended to me. I blamed my mother for not having the strength to put up a defense that would earn me some worth among them.

But after a few years of observation and fights, wherein I now became the one to defend her, I finally understood the position she was in and the fact that it would be more natural to sacrifice one soldier than an army. Suddenly, I turned my attention toward the curiosity of why my father was not present, and my mother told me her story that was filled with abusive memoirs and regrets. She assured me I was her joy even though she endured all that misery, but to me, I was more sympathized with rather than being loved.

I thought about everything she said that day and was trying to analyze what they had gone through with their decision. From that, I have concluded that my existence was not based on two people loving each other, so then it must be for a purpose; it was hard trying to comfort myself with the belief I was not a mistake and trying to accept the reality. After a few years, life became more difficult. I also learned that my father had a son, and he wanted us to get acquainted with each other. I was excited there was another that bore the same name as me.

Don't be judgmental because I love my other siblings, but I was more at peace and excited I was not alone bearing my name. After a few years, I learned that my brother had died, and the worst part of all was I never got to meet him. Somehow, I know he must have been excited too, looking forward to meeting his sister.

I thought life had given me more than it believed I could handle, but rather than mourning over my loads, I tried to make them more unimportant. From the stories they taught in Sunday school, there was one that caught my attention: it was the birth of Jesus Christ and the purpose of his existence.

I thought long and hard that day after church and understood that our destiny was created before our existence. Suddenly my loads became lighter, and that was one story that affected my life to accept the Lord as my savior. I have forgiven all who have hurt me and appreciate all things good or bad, understanding that they have played their path in me finding my strength.

At times, I felt forsaken by my father, but through my abandonment, I was adopted by the hands of God. And if death had stolen my only companion, I had found a friend and brother in Jesus Christ. At times, I would lean upon my understanding when I was feeling lost and defenseless, but I had the choice to serve the God that created all things. He has blessed me with the Holy Spirit, which becomes my guide, my armor, and comfort.

My journey has shown me right and wrong. Often, I have come face to face with death, sometimes earned by choices I have made along the way. Life has even brought me to the lowest of the lowest, to a point where I thought my position was my resting place. I refused to stay down because I have seen myself as one of God's greatness. I believe that if we are of his creation, then we shall exceed greatness by his will. Nothing is impossible for him to do, so why should we be dismayed or worried? When all we have to do is ask secretly, openly exalt his presence, and receive in abundance, not only knowing the truth but also living by the truth.

One of the most gifts God has granted us with is the ability to make our own choices. I have taken that choice to forgive all and grow to see my self-worth within God's creation. We all were given the power to be happy or unhappy. I'm no different from any other, and I have had my share of hardship and disappointment. However, I would choose the pathway of restoration, with the acceptance there will still be battles and afflictions but with the belief and faith my God will never forsake me.

There's a Thin Line Between to Create and to Destroy

> The heart is deceitful above all things, and desperately wicked: who can know it? I the LORD search the heart, I try the reins, even to give every man according to his ways, and according to the fruit of his doing.
>
> —Jeremiah 17:9–10

I was always willing to help a brother or sister, whether they are a child of God or not, because I never practiced partiality with deeds. I never ashamed to share my downfalls and victories with anyone because the testimony of anyone's experiences is an inspiration and an insight that all is not lost. But with all things, it brings good and evil.

I had a friend in Christ. I knew her from when I was a young teen; she was my mother's friend from her place of worship. I knew of her as a woman of God, doing God's will with obedience. Because of traveling, I was not in touch with her. I asked about her, keeping her in prayers. My mother didn't know of her whereabouts or what had happened to her, either.

One day, my mother called to say she has contacted her, and based on my mother's information, she was not in a good position; she needed help. Immediately I asked my mother to send my number to her so I could see how I can provide support. She called and spoke about all the afflictions taking place within her life and expressed she would like to travel to where I was to seek a new life for herself.

She even added that God had offered revelation that with this help, it would also open doors for a place of worship where she would serve as the pastor. Honestly, I was healing from a betrayal, but because I knew of her as a woman of God, I never hesitated to help, knowing I would have to share my home and provide for her until she could get a job. With the belief that God would stand with me, I told her yes. She should prepare to travel; I would stand as her refuge.

I took her as my family and provided as if she was one of my children. If I wrote about the ordeal of this experience, it would be a whole book. When I couldn't understand or explain her actions and those which my kids have shared, I would call my mother to give me answers. Each time I look back on those days and smile to myself, my kids made fun of me because before her arrival, I offered a lecture on who she was and what she represented, and they viewed a different character. I laugh to myself. The last thing she did was make a false accusation against me.

She made a story, telling my friend and her husband I had put her out in the street in the cold. They took her in; they expressed their concern and view on the matter to the extent they placed judgment on me without cause. Her actions did not hurt me because others have shown me gratitude with unkindness, but what surprises me is that she had done all these things as she displayed to the world she was a woman of God.

Her doing could have broken my belief. I had placed her on high grounds because of who she represented. "If she had chosen to step on the grounds of immorality, how does she still speak in tongues and utter what the Lord says?" I asked my mother.

But she replied, "Thus saith the Lord of Hosts, Hearken not unto the words of the prophets that prophesy unto you: they make you vain: they speak a vision of their own heart, and not out of the mouth of the Lord" (Jeremiah 23:16).

Admittedly, I will not escape the affliction of evil men, but God will never allow them to take my life because he is my protector, refuge, strength, and most of all, the source of my life. I will say to you, as I would say to myself, never allow the evil of humankind to change your course and purpose of being who you are and what you should represent as a human.

The heart is a place of love when broken. Allow your heart to mend with forgiveness, as we all have been down the pathway of pain, dishonesty, and despair, rather than restore these emotions with revenge. Be the one to give light on the value of which we should be living and allow ourselves to step away from the circle of destruction. Always remember to be a creator of love, and be sure that your heart is not mended with scars of any hostility.

Humbleness of a Man Will Direct His Path

Humble yourself, therefore, under the mighty hand of God, that he may exalt you in due time.
—1 Peter 5:6

Many characterize themselves as being humble based on their good deeds; some say that they're respectful for the success, opportunity, or birthrights that were given or bestowed upon them. Others are deprived by either discrimination or misfortunes under the submission of humbleness. But I will remind you that to be humble is to be meek because the worth of success nor poverty doesn't define your character.

Honestly, I never thought of myself being better than anyone, maybe because growing up, I was often deprived of many opportunities, where I was made humble by misfortune, so I never obliged to do so. Growing up and being on my journey of life, I never departed from that sense of humbleness; I even deprived myself when giving to another. Many say I was allowing myself to be too meek, and that's the reason others had the chance to cause me afflictions.

But being humble throughout my life has bestowed favor an increase in my doing. There are times I stand face to face with my opponent without fear. Knowing that with the help from my creator, I will defeat the purpose with humility, making my enemies my friends, as I resist all judgment with humility, as it allows me to overcome afflictions without injuries.

And I have also seen where my humbleness has taken me to sit with those of honor. It also has taken me places I never dreamed of going and allowed me to endure gracefully. Even with my choice of submission to God, it has granted me the purpose of writing these words within this book, telling you about his grace and reminding you of his will and promises and love for humanity.

Humbleness not only directs your pathway of life, but it also creates an atmosphere of purity with families, partners, and friends. We are all human, and we only react to the emotions one gives; without control, we are driven to anger, where our response defeats a whole purpose. I have been a victim and also a culprit because I am not perfect. By recognizing the wrongs, I have brought myself to surrender to apply uprightness and humility to humanity.

By finding the value of self-worth within myself, I have also required the ability of independence by learning to control my own emotions, happiness, battles, and destiny with the choices which I made. Applying humbleness within your household with the submission of modesty to your partner will create excellent communication skills that will also bring respect and gratitude to each other.

With parenting, humbleness should play a very vital role in the upbringing of a child. By applying that effect, it will bring acceptance and consent, mainly when the household consists of young adults. To be humble is not to less of oneself nor being silent but to reveal the divine presence within us as we represent our creator in every action and revelation of his truth without confusion. With that, the innocence of humanity would suddenly replenish itself.

Music Is a Non-Racist Weapon

And above all these things put on charity, which
is the bond of perfectness.

—Colossians 3:14

I was born and raised in Kingston, Jamaica. Music was, and still is, the life force of the people in Jamaica. Within my community every weekend, there would be a dance party, with trendy fashion and titles for the event. The promoters would organize a sound system to play they selective genre of music, chosen by the DJ selectors. I was never permitted to attend these parties by my mother because I was a child, and as a teen, my request was denied without words.

But I would stay up that weekend at my window, enjoying the selected music from the DJs from the sound systems such as Stone Love, Bass Odyssey, and JamRock—those were the top sound systems. Those were my times of enjoyment. Some nights, my brother and sister would join in, but eventually, they would fall asleep. I had no preference within my musical choices, but I was always intrigued by musical words and tunes of freedom, love, truth, and unity.

I can remember in the nineties in Kingston, Jamaica, they were feuds or wars around the communities. Some say the type of music brings cause to the wars; others say it was just political affairs. But from observation, I think it was more political because people would gather dancing and enjoying the music without segregation of their political names.

But the younger generation has taken music to a different level. Some would argue that music is expressive thoughts and feelings, but to those who wrote musical tunes of poverty, rivals, and political preference, I would say to you why not write it in a theme that will bring forth positive changes in how it will affect you and those listening?

When I traveled and could enjoy the company of others and their music, I was astonished by how they would sound just like my countrymen. When given the challenge to sing reggae music, even if they were of a different race, without facial recognition, I would say that sound was from a Jamaican.

Music within humanity is a life force that enslaves everything in its path without racism, a contagious vibe that never fails to spread its musical tunes to our hearts and minds. Music stands on its own, flowing without a form of segregation or with hatred. It never displaces humanity; it only displays the culture of its ancestry.

Many have tried continuously aiming to corrupt the essence of its devotion by molding lyrics of hatred, condemnation, and persecution, by composing spirit anthems of genocides. Love is the conception of humanity, and music is the delivery within our birth, aid, and peace, never to be composed of indifference but to create love and unity within this world.

Musically we were created, and by the music, we shall communicate, with love, togetherness, and with strength. The strength that unifies us as a people of one world is created in a musical world; every creature and element has its symbolic melodies that alert its atmosphere with sounds of vigilance, readiness, and seductive harmony.

Humanity is gifted with the sounds of praise that symphonize and unify us as worshippers before God by recognizing his presence and creation. Without impurity, we were born, and so should we be living; with grace, we should embody God's healing, a natural mechanism of healing that created within us. A spiritual life force that comforts emotions and brings togetherness. Why should we not, as a people, place the same concept that music brings, of many sounds that harmonize without recognition of any color, which brings forth visions of love and peace to all?

The Creator Affirms Life and Death

Peace I leave with you, my peace I give unto you:
not as the world giveth, give I unto you. Let not
your heart be troubled, neither let it be afraid.
—John 14:27

My grandmother's youngest child, Anthony, whom we all call Uncle Tony, is the smallest but the one with the biggest heart and the hustler out of all the siblings. We all had our times of asking for support from him. No matter the cause, he never hesitates to help. He always had a smile on his face, one that could light up the darkest room, and always strove to bring togetherness within the family and those around him.

His occupation was many; he was born to hustle. Still, for a few years, he continued to do his business selling fresh fish in the market, and he was delighted in what he did. He succeeded in his business, and customers loved him because of his personality. He was also an aid to those that were in need, and always gave with a loving heart.

Two years ago, my uncle mysteriously went crazy; I heard that someone tampered with his smoke. But within my uncle's illness, I could see the indifference shown to him. It is sad to say that you must trigger people's memories for them to show compassion to others. My uncle went missing, so I took it upon myself to search for him. I even asked those who knew of his whereabouts, but I failed with my search, and it had been weeks, and I hadn't seen or heard of him.

One night as I was home, my neighbor knocked on my door, letting me know there was a crazy man at the gate asking after me.

Instantly, I dashed around her and saw my uncle Tony standing there with his smile as usual. I take him in, allowed him to take a shower, and gave him fresh clothes and food. I told him I would take care of him, and he should never give up hope.

He smiled and said, "I know you will, my niece. Do you know that you are my favorite?"

"Yes, I do, and the feeling is mutual."

He laughed as he played with the kids. I offered for him to stay that night because I had prepared for him at a Drug and Mental Institute at the government hospital to see if they could help him. He asked me to allow him to return in the morning. Honestly, I was worried that he wouldn't make it back, but as I knew him to be a man of his word, so I agreed, with strict instructions to meet me at the bus stop at 7:00 a.m.

At around 6:30 that morning, I was already there waiting. I sat there till 8:00 a.m., and there was no sign of him. I started to worry, then half an hour later, I saw him running toward me with a bag under his arms. Breathlessly, he tried to explain that he stopped by my mother's house to get a bag for his clothes, and he also woke up late. He spent six weeks within the institution, and he has recovered from his sickness.

A lot had happened after his release, but around that time, I was traveling for work. Still, I was getting updates on him from my family. He was out in the street again, and this time, he had gotten HIV from his shared needles. I visited a couple of times, and that time was his happiest and mine. We went everywhere together. I tried to fulfill all his requests. On one trip, returning to work a few weeks after, I got a phone call that my uncle Tony was dead.

No one could believe that a person with such heart would live a life of confusion and pain, but one thing I was happy for was that, within his sickness, he had given his life to God, and that was what brought peace to me.

Life or death! Which is more fearsome? Many of us would say death because no one wishes to die, and others may speak of death as a solution to the hardship and misfortune they are experiencing.

By affirming that God is our creator, you will also declare the diversity of his creation, not only for the worldly things but also for the reality of life and death. Life brings the existence of humanity, and death brings grief, but it also brings awareness and respect to life. I would say it's an eye-opener to the acceptance of what life is worth. Death is the only force that brings us back to the essence of our beliefs in God.

People say death brings separation, but I believe it creates togetherness for those that have ceased to communicate and show love toward others. My grandmother hated my concept of death because of fear. I understand her concerns, but why fear what is essential to creation? I believe that if you accept the Lord God as your savior and try to live a life of righteousness, it will surely offer an everlasting life after death.

Inspire Me to Love with Devotion

Let all that you do be done in love.

—1 Corinthians 16:14

Love only has one meaning, but we all have different ways of express-ing our feelings about love. It is so easy for us to express our emo-tions, but the real importance is how committed you are to your actions and to allow what you share to be meaningful.

I did not know which direction I should go with the quote because it speaks of love, loyalty, and commitment. But I will start by expressing the love I have for God, of which I do so often within this book. To love God is to fear God, not in the sense of horror but of respect and honor. If I were only to share the love I have for God and not for my mother and father, then I would be a biased person. God's love does not come with partiality, so I can't be loving God and not show respect and honor to my parents.

As I was growing up in my stepfather's house, the indifference around was not only physically but also felt. I wish my mother could have been more of a defense in times of abuse. When I went around to my other families, they would have this pity reaction toward me from what they knew. I could not understand why my father was never around, and I was his only child at the time before I knew from my aunt he had a son, who died at fifteen years old.

My mother could not fight my battles, but I never hated her for what she could not do. My mother was never a hugger, and she rarely expressed her love through emotions, so as a child, I was never sure how to approach her with issues. My father never existed, and my stepdad always had a wave of anger anytime I am around. The physical and mental abuse got to a point where I needed answers, and the only person I could get it from was my mother, so one day, as she was sitting at the front porch, having her relaxation time, I decided that I would ask why everyone hated me.

She looked at my face and expressed she had never hated me and never would, and that was when my mother let me know what had happened between her and my father. She spoke about her pain and abuse from my father that night he molested her, the battle she endured, and the choices she regretted making. She regretted she told no one about the abuse, and after a month, she discovered that she was pregnant, and both my grandmothers settled it their way without the police involvement.

All this information was too much to bear, but I finally received an answer to why I received these emotions from others and why I was never any worth to my father. At that young age, you would think that I could never deal with knowing I was a child produced by rape, but even as a child, my thoughts were as deep as a pit. I admire my mother even more because she could have decided not to bring me to this world. But she took the responsibility and the shame that comes with it and try to protect and love me the best way she knew.

I have offered forgiveness and love to my father, and even though I could not figure out why my stepdad treats me with abuse, I still offer forgiveness to him. Today, my mother is my best friend, and I honor her for the pride she walks with even though it is a shame to others. The love, loyalty, and commitment she showed to me and the promises she made to be by my side even when the battle was too hard for her to fight.

She stood with me with the little she had; honestly, I felt no type of hate toward those who offer abuse because I try to have more profound thoughts on people's actions and emotions. And I believe that the resentment and hurt one feels is replaceable with the devotion of God's love, so I will never see them with hate.

Even though we are living in a world of good and evil, one should not allow his interest to be captivated by the immoralities that wanders around us. As humans, we should be able to offer the same love and devotion God offers to us. Who I am is what God created, and I will never see myself as a circumstance, and neither should you. We should all learn to love without condition and regrets, and we must be able to see the importance of being humane with devotion.

Great Minds Hunted by Procrastination

He that observeth the wind shall not sow; and he
that regardeth the clouds shall not reap.
—Ecclesiastes 11:4

Humanity was created by greatness and filled with creativity. As we dominated this world with visions and desires, many of us been favorable to demonstrate and share our abilities with others. Still, there are some that lack the determination or even battle with doubt within themselves. We are our own enemy, depriving not only our dreams to become a reality but also the world from the greatness that bestowed upon us; with no beliefs within ourselves, we prevent our manifestation of becoming inventors, educators, leaders, and advisors.

I did not know that I would be here writing this book, having the capability to inspire others, as I open to the acceptance of who I am and the life path chosen for me. Even with fear, I still pursue this task given onto me. With all my pains and struggles, I was still able to either use the testimonies of my battles to elevate my broken spirit and even remind myself that I am worthy of all that's before me.

When I was a child, you could find me in a corner with plain paper and pencil, sketching objects or writing stories. Those were my means of fun or my ways of escaping from what was happening around me. Many may ask, how is it possible to see positivity within a negative path? But with all the positivity, this world will never be the same without the negativity that lingers around us. One that remains the most and always against us is procrastination. It feeds upon our willpower by creating a diversion. Many of us being tormented with the spirit of procrastination, which drives us to delay possibilities of visions and inspirations that could make a change within us or in the life of someone else.

As our minds are captivated by idling pleasures, we become doubtful and loses faith within ourselves. These possibilities will bring regrets, as we wonder if maybe those dreams could have made a difference within humanity and even within ourselves. Big or small, the sizes of ideas do not affect the impact it possesses; what you should do is to unleash your mind from thoughts of rejection and fears.

Individually, we were all created equal and possess the abundance of greatness to achieve all our desires. But it's within ourselves we choose either to unfold or to conceal our abilities. By believing within ourselves, this will open the access we need to uncover our passion and beliefs that we have to contribute. We all need inspiration for us to achieve; we also need to offer encouragement as a form of strength. Many men and women overcome fears to pursue greatness, and I have lived by the words of those who set a pathway for others to follow.

"And as we let our light shine, we unconsciously give other people permission to do the same," said Nelson Mandela.

"The greatness of a man is not in how much wealth he acquires, but in his integrity and his ability to affect those around him positively," said Bob Marley.

"Faith is taking the first step even when you don't see the whole staircases" (Martin Luther King Jr).

My hope is that individuals young and old are not to fear the unknown in an attempt in expression or creativeness. To either share your thoughts and dream with the rest of the world, we may not reach a thousand. Still, even a hundred will bring significance and fulfillment to what God has bestowed upon us by knowing we have done our purpose, contributing to humanity itself. Because I believe "There's no limitation to what humanity possesses, but the battle is getting to know our values."

I have always yearned for the possibilities that could change this world from its immoralities that affiliate itself with humanity, knowing that one person can never possess such capabilities. However, still, I hope my attempt would change or encourage someone's life. The love and admiration I have for humanity comes from what I see, the capabilities we possess, the value of our existence, and the will-power we own that can turn any dream to become a reality

Life Offers Uncertainty, While Faith Arise by Grace

Not that we are sufficient of ourselves to think anything as of ourselves; but our sufficiency is of God.

—2 Corinthians 3:5

When my children were five and nine years old, I traveled to the Turks and Caicos Islands to work on a three-year contract; that three years turned into nine years. I always strive to give my kids the best, so being away from them was my great sacrifice to do so. I hardly see my kids, and it was hard, but I reminded myself it was for a greater purpose. As time went by, they were achieving and performing well academically, and they made me proud. But when my son stepped into his adolescent age, issues arose, and my mother could not handle him on her own; she called to say that it was time for me to come home.

I suddenly chose the child rather than the money at this point. I wasn't even thinking about how I would continue schooling them at the level they were. I resigned from my job, and everyone was asking if I was making the right decision; even I asked myself that question. I went back to Jamaica, not sure how I would survive because of my absence. The money I came with was enough to buy a home, but I considered starting a business instead. Even though I knew it would be tough starting up a business in a place where you have not lived for almost ten years, and to add to that issues, my kids didn't want to stay.

I would honestly say as a single parent, your only source dependent is God. I had to make all the choices of every means, whether it's good or bad. After a couple of months, I lost every dime I own. At this time, I finally considered making a move but this time with my kids, because I promised them never to leave them behind again. But it wasn't all my decision. My teen and preteen had their say, but my rules were, "If we go and we become homeless, hungry, I don't want to hear any cries."

My daughter's words were "Mommy we got God with us." My son said, "You always tell us to live by faith." I smiled, and I didn't say another word.

I allow my kids to make their own decision, but I always remind them there are still circumstances that come along with every choice. There were my kids, so you know they were going to hit with some verse from the bible or words of inspiration, and honestly, I was between a rock and a hard place, so there was no turning back.

I could tell you that from the day we left Jamaica, by the grace of God, we never experienced being homeless or ever felt hungry any day. Every step of the way with perseverance and faith, God fulfilled every promise he made to us by doing his will through those that have shared their homes, food, and love with us until we were able to do the same for others. I wrote these words with no doubt. I have been a living testament to God's promises; I have ceased to wait on his doing and regret my steps. Many have stopped believing simply because they have not seen the face of God. But from what I know and experience, the God I serve is a divine spirit.

The essence of such can take on any image; each time I see an act of kindness or an act of solidarity, I see God in all these doings. Remember that life and everything else as its cycle and purpose, every nature has its seasons and a time for every doing, and even in that time, I still see the act of God. I have spent my life working toward his favor and taken heed of his commandments, presenting myself as a living sacrifice at the altar of his presence.

The accomplishment of his grace which he had shown my kids and me each day, the steadfast protection and the provider he is to us gives me the authority to take on life tasks and struggles without fear or doubts. Knowing that my steps are ordered, I still have confidence no matter how often I have fallen or lose hope. I never cease to place God at the threshold of my life; as he offers his grace and mercy sufficiently toward me.

Living Life with Persistence Determines Prosperity

And I say unto you, Ask, and it shall be given you; seek, and ye shall find; knock, and it shall be opened unto you. For every one that asketh receiveth; and he that seeketh findeth, and to him that knocketh it shall be opened.
—Luke 11:9–10

For me to write about persistence, I would have to go through battles for you to believe that with endurance comes prosperity, and I think that life can test your faith. When I traveled away from my kids to fulfill their needs and education, it was a hard choice, but we must do what seems right in time of desperation. Everything started great for a while, and my kids attended the best schools. Despite my absence, I was comforted by smiles and results by their performance.

It was a back-to-school season, and their payment was two hands full; before then, my work season got slow, and I didn't want to take any loan from my boss. I was so doubtful in my mind that at one point, I was about to change their school, but I was determined to let them continue because I believe when a child gets an early stable start in their life, it will help to create strong foundations.

I moved out of my apartment again so I could be able to provide the money I needed for them to continue their education and also their other needs. I had moved in with a friend, but the accommodation got uncomfortable. As soon as she tells me that her boyfriend didn't like the idea, her complaint did not seem right because he wasn't living there, so she used him as an excuse. But without objection, I packed my stuff and left her house. Without malice, I genuinely thanked her for the few days because I realize that sometimes, others can be a form of a test within your life.

I didn't want to intrude anyone after that comment my friend made; I refused to let anyone else felt that way. I sat in the car and prayed and lived in my car for the time until I clear my bills. I could tell you that never anyone gets that I was living on the road because I never wear my dismay on my face. It was the last two weeks in August, and I sent my kids tuition and cover all their expenses, except for upkeep. Now I planned that with the next two weeks' pay, I would have to send money for their maintenance and then continue to live out here till I get enough money to get the apartment.

The month was slow, so I wasn't expecting a commission for the month, but to my surprise that Saturday, my boss handed me my check and said, "You always hit the commission." I was surprised; as I was walking away, he calls me back. He gave me a few dollars and said it was from him and his wife for the kids to help them back out to school because they knew I was a single parent. I told him "Thanks." I was so grateful that day. I had enough money to send home and at least a month's rent budget to get a new place.

I went to have dinner that night, and I was there chatting with a friend. He told me there was a place he knew for rent; I took the information and called her. I told her I don't have the two months' rent, but with surprise, she accepts what I had. I went into the house that same day. The only thing I needed was to get my light credit for it to turn on, but that was the least. I lived in that house for a week without natural light but never felt I was in the dark because the light which shone through me was an everlasting light that will never fade. My God has favored me every step of the way.

Each possesses the willpower to take life as an adventure, and there would always be desires that give us the tenacity to go hard against its numerous obstacles. In every aspect of our lives, determine hard work and persistence to achieve all our desires. One act of endurance was carrying the responsibilities of being a single mother; it was not by my choice but the reaction from choices I made without thoughts. We have all made thoughtless decisions, all in the name of love or needs.

Under these influences, we respond carelessly by our actions and choices. In my defense against these choices I had made, I never allowed them to be a compass of direction along the rest of my journey. But I never admit defeat in anything I do, and I also know that life can be cruel with its harvest. But the significant reason for living is that it allows you to fail then gives you enough purpose to rise again.

Life is good! And the abundance of life is there for us to experience, even though it's full of diversity and the battles are unbearable. Still, if we apply perseverance with persistence, it will render the fulfillment of which life as to offer. For us to pursue with persistence, our faith would have to be stimulated spiritually by the word of God, by knowing he is the source of all things and desires.

In Everything We Do Lies Truth

My children let us not love in word, neither in tongue; but indeed, and in truth.
—1 John 3:18

For every truth in life, one has to reflect on the journey that brings it to acceptance.

Worshippers' truth relies on the importance of our beliefs. If I say I am a child of God, I am declaring that I should uphold righteousness. You may ask what gives me the right to affirm this identity, and I will tell you, "Obedience." Because salvation is already secured, but the pathway to it relies on your obedience. For me, as a worshipper, I need to seek and live by the words of God, and that brings submission. Submission is the law, and I can say it is difficult because as humans, we don't even submit to those that stand before us.

But the most significant thing about this submission is that it's not by force. The last thing we need to be able to worship in truth is the Holy Spirit, to stand as our guide and connection to God. And devotion is where the growth of love and loyalty is practiced, and commitment allows you to see your creator, and that will create in you a worshiper who not only worships but worships in Spirit and in truth.

Forgiveness truth—an act of showing compassion and also to relieve us from the burdens which create vengeance within our heart, which can create obstacles within our path of prosperity. I have forgiven my mother for not standing between me and my afflictions as a child, simply because she never knew how to. I have forgiven my stepdad for allowing himself to be used to demonstrate acts of cruelty toward me. I have also forgiven my father for his choice of selfishness, allowing me to dwell within the arms of abandonment and afflictions because I was fatherless. Forgiveness removes burdens and grieves, and it brings an energy of upliftment, success, peace, and uprightness within your life.

Life truth—giving consent to its cycles of changes, accepting that life and time is the master of all things. Believing that anything that is broken can be fixed and with hard work, all levels of life are changeable with determination, which brings success and favor to those which attack life obstacles with perseverance and faithfulness. My favorite phrase is "No man position in life is permanent," because with determination brings levels of changes within a person's life. Just as time defines life, I also believe "What you sow is what you reap." And as sowers, we don't get the opportunity to reap, and our children become the reapers of what we sow, whether it's good or bad, so be careful what you sow.

Faith truth—the reality of our beliefs in who we are, the fountain of strength and the meaning of living life not by what but in what we hope and desire, which confirm our beliefs. "Knowing who I am and the God that I serve have given me enough evidence to live by His words and promises" (Hebrews 11:1). My sister always said when she feels defeated and loses her belief, she thinks about how I have demonstrated a life of faith daily in everything I do, which restores her strength in times of her defeat.

Growing up experiences have taught me that the only dependence I needed was on God, but as we know, life comes with obstacles. And believing in yourself and with assurance from God will elevate your beliefs in a time of doubt, and always remind yourself, "I am for God and not against Him."

Humanity truth—all the above, and to see beyond our differences by creating a union that stands as a tower of strength that can never break in times of afflictions, disasters, and griefs. I have found the love of God within myself because I have accepted who God is, and by knowing who he is, you will also know who you are representing and the authority which you hold as a child of God. And we should all show appreciation by celebrating the values of our existence, giving honor and worship to our creator, exalt his doing by giving glory onto him for that is all required of us as humans.

At the Threshold of Death, Life Becomes Golden

I cried to thee, O LORD; and unto the LORD
I made supplication. What profit is there in my
blood when I go down to the pit? Shall the dust
praise thee? shall it declare thy truth.
—Psalm 30:8–9

December 5, 2013, I was home doing my house chores when suddenly I felt a sharp pain on the right side of my abdomen. It went as fast as it comes, but after a few more times, it slowly became unbearable, and I decided to drove to the hospital. Upon reaching the hospital, the pain got worse. I usually can tolerate my pain, but at this time, I was about to fail. As the nurse was examining me and asked the gravity of pain I was in, I told her a 10. She smiled and said, "That's impossible, you are still standing."

"This is all pride," I replied.

The doctors came in to assist me; they did their examination, but from my observation, I think they were as confused as I was about my condition. I asked them to give me some morphine, but still, I felt no relief, and I asked for more, but the pain was on the same level. I was just about to get some sleep, when I heard a familiar voice within the room. It was my gynecologist, Dr. Page. She was surprised to see it was me and asked what all the fuss was about. She showed her concern and expressed she would do everything to help me.

It had been hours, and I felt my body shutting down section by section. My body was telling me it could not contain this pain anymore and it was giving up on me. My vision was blurry, and the room felt as if it was moving in a circle. I was alone. Still, I could feel a strange presence in the room with me. The energy it gave off didn't feel right. It was a feeling of peace but on a deeper level, one I knew I would never return from. At this moment, I spoke to God as if he were standing there holding my hands.

"God, it seems as if death is here, and I am not afraid for myself but my children. Still, if it is of your will that I should go with the spirit of death, I will rest assured that you have already prepared another to pick up where I left off to offer guidance to them." I was ready to give up because I could not take it anymore.

As I was lying there, I was in and out of consciousness. My nurse noticed and call my doctor. She returns and takes me to do another ultrasound. She explained that she would operate to get a better idea of what was going on inside. The nurse got me ready for surgery. She then suggested that I sign a consent form to begin. The last thing I could remember going into the surgery was my doctor asking me how I felt.

After surgery, I woke up, and I felt as if I were strapped to the bed. I tried to move, but I was in pain. I look down on my stomach covered with a bandage, and I was attached to different IVs. A nurse watching me asked me if I was feeling okay. I told her I was in pain. She left and returned with Dr. Page followed by another doctor I never saw during that night. They both smiled as they approached my bed. "I can see that you are awake," said Dr. Page. This is Dr. Sam—he is your surgeon." He smiled and nodded. Then he asked me when the last time I had fish.

I was a little bit confused by the question, then I remembered, "I had fish like six days ago," I replied. They look at each other, and then Dr. Sam explained that they found a fishbone; he expressed I could not have swallowed a bone that size and not feel it.

Dr. Sam continues to explain that the fishbone went down my chest into my stomach, and as it was passing through the intestine, the bone ruptured the organ. He expresses he doesn't know how I was alive at this moment. "It was God," said Dr. Page. Both smiled and agreed. They handed me a small bottle with this bone, Dr. Page suggested that I keep this bone close and that this should be a lesson to all these fish lovers.

That night, as I lay in the hospital bed, I reflected on everything they said. I felt grateful for the work they had performed on me to save my life. I reflected on my choices, failures, regrets, happiness and my kids. I asked myself, *Why I am not dead? What's the reason for this excess breath of life that has been given to me? Was it for my children, or is it for a purpose?* I have been a living testament to what God can do in your life. I had seen where he turned the stone in which the builder refuses to be the head cornerstone and where he had chosen life for me when I thought I would be dead.

Seek Righteousness to Appreciate the Abundance of Life

⬱⬱⬱

Blessed are they which do hunger and thirst after righteousness: for they shall be filled.
—Matthew 5:6

For one to call himself righteous, he also proclaims that he is a divine being, and no human can stand in such devotedness or honor. If one tries to pursue righteousness, he declares he's a man of dignity, fairness, and morals, which is the duty of humanity.

I have proclaimed the name of God upon myself and wear it as an identity. Am I claiming that I am righteous? No! But I am declaring that I am striving toward living a life of righteousness. Throughout my journey, in the beginning, I was alone with the mindset I would do all to survive because God helps those who help themselves. With no guidance from a father figure, you can already see I was heading for trouble.

When I felt I was at the age of dating, I dated only older men. My friends teased me a lot, saying I was searching for my father. But I have made my choices, and whatever the circumstances, I decided to live with it, no matter what it was. I was never living a life of righteousness because I never knew how to. I was serving two masters as a convenience. I was going places, and my hustle had been profitable.

But what I noticed was that no matter what I achieved, it did not bring fulfillment. My mind and heart were not in a state of completion; neither was I to enjoy what was around me entirely. Each time I complained about this void within me to my friends, they would say I had little sense because I had all that they wanted and I was not happy; they couldn't understand what I was feeling.

I also stood as the head of my household because I was a single parent, and even if I convinced myself to have a relationship, I would still be on that path as if I inherited it. I didn't bring what was happening outside into my home among my children because I got very territorial with my kids. But even though it never exposed to them, I knew I was not living a life of a good example, the life I tried to illustrate to them of moral standard.

As a single parent, we try to do all we can to provide for our children, forgetting that we are being watched, and being the head of the household doesn't give you the right not to give concern on how you make the impossible possible. Even though you try your best to hide the hustle, you will never be at peace with yourself. Allow God to do the hustle for you instead. I am not saying you should sit and fold your arms but make wise choices of which you can be proud to say, "I did, and I survived."

Also, as the head of your house is not about having control or power over your family. It is not only to be a source for needs, wants, or desires but mainly to be the main instrument used by God to open the hearts of your family to righteousness. These ethics should not only be displayed among our household but also to others, which would define our character to society. As we demonstrate our deeds of righteousness, we're also constructing a reputation which can open doors of opportunity without bonds, but never forget the cycles of critiques, slandering, expectation, and evaluation from others. Always try to live your life with uprightness before God and the people, as we are not bonded within our situation and sins because it is changeable.

To Worship Is to Exalt, to Suppress Is to Deny

Ask of me, and I shall give thee the heathen for thine inheritance, and the uttermost parts of the earth for thy possession.

—Psalm 2:8

I'll never cease to let others know that my life path is a living testimony to what God has promised. That's why I exalt him with every chance I get and declare that he's the only true and reigning God.

At a young age, I have served God as my savior without understanding, stepping on a pathway of which I have no experience or knowledge of its expectation. On that day, my choice could have been for many or one reason; no matter my reason for making that decision, in my heart, I knew the road would never be easy for such gifts and promises. But still, I accepted the journey, unaware of all the unexpected battles and victories, success, and failures, hate, and love, of which I've already seen.

As my journey continues without guidance, my beliefs become doubtful because of the affliction and choices I had to make to survive. I have fallen often, and temptations wrestle with me endlessly. But in the midst of this, my God has shown me mercy despite my transgressions. He offers me the favor of grace even though I am not worthy of such, and even as I walk through the valley of death, he has never forsaken me or handed me over to the hands of death.

I have worshiped the Lord thy God because he is worthy to be praised. He has seen beyond my faults because of he who has made me. My choices have brought me good and bad results, but no matter the outcome, he offers forgiveness and assurance. He is a step ahead of me. I have found peace within my afflictions because he will never forsake me. My journey has not ended because I am alive and well, and for that, I will never cease to exalt his name for the goodness he as shown me, without expectation nor obligation because it is of my choice to worship him.

Often, death has shown me my unworthiness, but as I am about to walk gladly within damnation, God reminds me he has already paid my price with the blood of His Son, Jesus Christ. I can never deny what I know because the testimony of my existence gives a declaration he is in control. The forgiveness and love I offer to those that cause me pain is the same love that pours out on me daily. He is my source of happiness, strength, and my provider. He places a smile on my face each time I see my children. In my time of weakness, I have regained my strength from the promises he made.

God is a god of understanding, patience, and love, which he offers us each day. Humanity! We should place him back where he belongs, not on the throne because he has never been removed but in a place within our hearts and our lives. We created to manifest within every area of our lives but never without his presence, remember that he is our Alpha and Omega, our Beginning, and our End. To show love and kindness to each other is our purpose as humans, to give praise and honor is our duty, but to cast judgment is only by God's doing.

Individuals we praise, but in unity, we worship, which creates world healing and prosperity for all. Wisdom should be seen with age because life offer cycles to be passed down as knowledge. And leaders should offer mercy because you are under the authority of God, and we are much so responsible for those we lead as we are for ourselves. Humanity, we should trust in the Lord thy God and "Know ye that the LORD he is God. It is he that hath made us, and not we ourselves; we are his people, and the sheep of his pasture" (Psalm 100:3).

Let us humble ourselves and never deny him in any situation. Let us willingly give praise unto him, as he is the unseen God, who graces our presence with his Divine Spirit. Let us welcome his spirit with truth and submission, as we give up our bodies as a vessel to be used by his will and utterance for humanity and his glory.

Wholeness Is Completeness
as Death Affirms Vanity

And the peace of God, which passeth all understanding, shall keep your hearts and minds
through Christ Jesus.

—Philippians 4:7

On the 10th of December 2013, leaving that hospital, as I was home recovering from my surgery, I had the luxury of time to reflect on my life. From what I have just been through, it has caused me to view life differently, seeking its worth and completeness within my thoughts and actions. Before this incident, I was in a car accident that also nearly took my life along with others. So I think it was time for me to live with some spiritual fulfillment and meaning to see its worth.

"Life is for living," my elders would say.

"Life is too short, so why we don't just live?" the young at heart would utter as they venture with moments given.

I agree with both statements, but my liveliness would filter differently to say, "Life should be lived with wholeness." So I ask, how can I live life to completeness when we know death awaits us? Truthfully, I realize this is the time for some soul searching. Life is to live with wholeness, rather than with lacking effort; to be complete is to live a life beyond one's limitation, by avoiding structures of diversions from others and procrastination within ourselves.

I never want to seem as if life should be this intense feeling with overbearing obligations to fill; life is about the growth of happiness, love, accomplishment, deliverance, peace, and unity. But we see completeness by the acquirement of worldly thoughts and achievements rather than with the spirituality of mind, body, and soul, which I believe confirms wholeness. The negativity that life has shown me has brought awareness to what I am worth and my aim.

I have to emphasize purpose throughout this book because I think every life on earth is of meaning, and I genuinely think that we can enjoy being in the process of doing or pursuing our goals with fulfillment. "You are a jack of all trades," my mother would say, but to think of it, I have mastered none of them. Survival causes that I could say, because of my choice and afflictions, I could never achieve stability.

But now, death has allowed me to see life values, and it as also shown me how it can all be in vain. My first step to wholeness started when I chose to serve one master, and that is God. I refused to live within my limitations because of relationships, family, and survival. Those were my excuses and defenses when I was approached by the Spirit of God, not realizing that he who is God can also offer all that I have chosen to be an obstacle.

I see God's wholeness as "The Father, Son, and the Holy Spirit," a symbol of the trinity. And I have viewed human wholeness as "mind, body, and soul," which I believe is God's way of saying he has made us complete. For myself, I have taken the trinity of God and placed it upon myself, and that is where I have lived my life with wholeness. I evoked my mind with the words of God, which brings me confidence and assurance of who I am and who is for me. Then I have taken the body of Christ that offers everlasting life and offer my body to be a vessel for his purpose. And for wholeness, I am under submission by the Holy Spirit, which is the direct connection and utterance to my soul from God, which direct my steps to a life of completeness.

I beg for humanity to live with wholeness with God and within ourselves and among others. It will release us from brokenness, bondage, and guilt to a life of peace, fulfillment, and righteousness. As an individual, this will bring restoration, confidence, and freedom. Life is for living, and to live with wholeness is first to accept God, welcome his presence, ask him to intercede, and receive the purpose of which he has given unto you, and that I believe is wholeness.

Why Question My Ambition with Useless Critique

꧁ ꧂

Who art thou that judgest another man's servant?
To his own master he standeth or falleth. Yea, he
shall be holden up: for God is able to make him
stand.

—Romans 14:4

You may have been considering that I was a broken and abused child. Still, I can tell you I was more broken mentally than physically because sometimes, I would fight back physically trying to defend myself, but still, I would hold words of hate and of uselessness that has spoken over my life. My inability to fight back caused by inexperience because I was still a child. I have observed my mother going through her trials and have given thought to how I can prevent such submission all in the name of love.

I wish at times I could stand between her and her battles, but when I do, it makes matters worse because she is a dependent within her union or I quickly become the target. "So what to do in this case?" I asked. Time brings wisdom, and wisdom brings change, so with time, I break my mother's cycles of submission of battles and take heed of the submission of God, allowing him to be my source of everything.

I have always seen myself as someone with some importance. I believe that with all the struggle life has given me, it should never be seen only as endurance. I placed the words of God as my foundation rather than the ones others speak over my life.

Words are powerful, but determination moves mountains. I was not only enduring useless words but also, I was restricted from sources that would have affected my ability to succeed because I was a fatherless child. And others would only show emotions of sympathy when I asked for help to break the chains that have bonded me from completion. For me, it never was easy to overcome, and I am sure it is the same for all of us. Having control will not be easy, but it will help you to be grounded with your desires.

I have always believed if you have the sight to see the vision of who you are, then you have the willpower of its manifestation to its reality. One thing I learned through experiences is that the enemies are given the tools and power to see beyond who we are, and with all their might, they will never allow you to see what they have seen, much less enable you to reap from its manifestation, as they design distraction by creating a phase of events that will divert you from your purpose.

The passion I have toward life has been created by struggles, which molded me into this individual who never allows afflicting elements to stand between me and the gift that God has placed upon my life as my purpose. The negative forces of this world as they wish will take its shape into whatever could break you spiritually or physically, with depression that disguises itself as ways to redemption.

Ways of dealing with these critiques were achieved by growth, not only the development from being a child to adulthood but also from being fearful to being faithful. And that attribute is created by time and experience and beliefs, as growth depends on how well you suppress negatives elements that affect you. My strength developed when I knew more of my creator, and time has brought progress to his promises, which strengthens my beliefs.

For you to overcome elements of confusions, you would have to detach spiritually and mentally from those that being used as an attack against you. Many of which disguised as your spouse, siblings, friends, authorities, families, and your children. Allow the power of God to be in control by turning the order of destructions to become reverse favor upon your life.

Whatever your ambition or purpose, learn to own your dreams even before they become a reality. Place the creator of all things at the center of your journey, allow him to order your footstep, and the order of utterance when speaking against verbal partiality, oppressors, and evaluation of our fate. Today I live and stand only on his words because experiences have offered me wisdom; I now live my life by knowing what I am worth and what I am worth is defined by my creator.

Never Wear Your Past
as a Backpack

He health the broken in heart, and bindeth up
their wounds.
—Psalm 147:3

Your past has the power to determine the present if you allow it to
be the order of your pathway. Many say, "Let the past be the past."
But how can I when others say, "Never forget where you are coming
from"? Should I continually preserve the memories of disappointment or abuse as a boundary or as the center of my journey?

Here is one such ordeal I will share with you, which I have never
spoken about to anyone. I was around sixteen years old when this
had taken place. I had gotten my access papers from my mother, as
I call it, to go out with friends. All my classmates had boyfriends. I
was a newbie to this side of life. Their stories seemed crazy and fun in
some ways; they had gotten the opportunity to be out partying and
had the choice to experience womanhood at their age.

One day, while we were walking around town after school, they
hung out in the park with other friends. I stopped by the arcade to
window shop on the latest fashion since it was on the same pathway
to home. As I was there, gazing around, my eyes caught the attention
of a particular guy staring right back at me. He was standing with
others, but his attention fixed on me for reasons I don't know.

He approached where I was standing, and he introduced himself, and we talked for a while, then he gave me his number, we got
the chance to talk on the phone a few times when my parents weren't
home because we not allowed to use the phone. After a couple of

weeks, he asked me to have lunch with him, which I agreed to. As we were driving, he told me we would have lunch at his house. I went with the idea because I developed trust for him as a friend.

I thought the feeling was mutual, reason being I gave no consent to change the type of friendship we shared. Because I viewed the world without experience but only for a short period, what happened next changed my view. Suddenly, my friend attempted to kiss me, but I turned my head away, after which he tried again, and I decided it was time for me to leave. He apologized for his behavior, but when I let down my guard, he tried again. As I was getting ready to go, he pulled me down and instantly he tried to undress me. I fought back, but I failed. He slapped me, and from there, I was raped.

I said nothing to my mother when I went home because my mother told me I wasn't ready to have a boyfriend, which I didn't have, but she never knew about the friendship I had with this man. I took what happened and wore it as my cross; I blamed myself for being there at his house. Two years later, I was in a relationship where I was beaten and raped again by my boyfriend friend.

As I journey toward life, going up against the trials that decorated my path, the strength by which I endured has become weaker as my battle increase, unable to hold a focus of the life before me. They say, "What doesn't kill you make you stronger." But where does my strength come from? Should I shift my depression to meditations of happiness instead of dejection? Must I heal from the abuse that afflicts me mentally or physically by surpassing the feelings of vengeance and replace it with forgiveness for my offenders?

One way I have dealt with my past is to see it as a testament, something that I can speak of but never live by. I have had my share of abuse, disappointment, failures, and wins because the past is not only an experience of distress but also brings happiness, peace, and achievement. The other way I dealt with my past is through forgiveness, not only mercy to those that wronged me but forgiveness toward myself dealing with emotions of failure, incompetence, and the incapability of prevention and defending myself from abuse.

I would randomly share this experience with a stranger if their situation is similar, allowing them never to let what has happened define their happiness. I have turned my misguided choices to be my step of guidance with my decisions. I've used failures as a power to stimulate my will to accept the results of my desires and allow fear to move about without recognition.

No two individuals can never relate to the same story because, as our choices are different, so are our courses; I can never endure my sister's pain or create their sacrifices. One's strength relies on the capacity of one's beliefs; I can never accompany you on your journey without knowing where my path leads. I have challenged my past it may never be the reason for my failure to accept love or to give love. I rejected the burdens of which it chooses for me to bear. And I have lived knowing that my past creates insights of my doing, never to be blind sighted by regrets, determining to live the fulfillment of my life doing my purpose, without burden and loads of my past, and I hope you do too.

It's the Honor in Which You Served

❦

> For God is not unrighteous to forget your work
> and labour of love, which ye have shewed toward
> his name, in that ye have ministered to the saints,
> and do minister.
>
> —Hebrews 6:10

I heard of stories of men and women that had been on the battle-grounds of wars, some which have died in honor and others have lived to tell tales and reap the greatness of their labor, but there is one soldier I had the pleasure to meet and had him share his stories with me.

Mr. Zee (not his real name) was ninety-four years old when he shared his stories with me; I was filling in for his nurse for a couple of days while she went on a family emergency. At his age, he was so full of life and eager to do things on his own, to show he was still dependable on his strength, so my job for the few days was easy and knowledgeable with all the wisdom and stories he had shared with me.

One such story was about his time in World War II in 1939–1945. He added that his father had given his service on the battle-ground in World War I that lasted from 1914 to 1918. He was so honored to be from a bloodline of a great soldier with dignity; as he showered his dad with compliments, he straightened up with a big smile and salute. He continued to express how his dad prepared him and his brother to be on the battlefield of World War II, and without fear, they were up for the task with honor to serve their country.

As he expressed his values and loyalty to the task and what he had endured, his memory dragged him back to events that should have taken his life and of other soldiers, but with his effort and determination, it defeated the purpose with no life taken. However, he was a little broken from not receiving his honor, but this never changed his love of being a soldier.

After he serves his country, he then ventured into his career path as an educator for the young men and women, "our future nations," he stated. Still, his attribute as a soldier was needed. As I sit each day enjoying his humor, his perception of life, he accepts his roles with humbleness, but he possesses the strength of a lion. His bravery is of no measure and neither are his beliefs. I admire that he places God at the forefront of his life, and he's quite satisfied with who he is.

I looked at this human being with a grateful heart, thanking God for the opportunity to stand before such boldness; there's much more to the few words I've shared with you that can complete a whole book of love, adventures, bravery, strength, hope, and faith from this one honorable individual that stands before me. He may not have received his recognition at the appointed time from the officials. Still, life has honored this man with grace. He has touched the lives of every individual that crossed his path, including me, and I admire and salute you, Mr. Zee, as an honorable soldier of humanity which you still served.

Either you are a soldier of war or a soldier of life; both tasks require endurance. The purpose and expectation we have entering in battles is to win, and at times, the results we get do not measure up to the sacrifices we offer. Many would say life is unfair, but neither can I justify what it offers. But I would also believe that once you step on these battlegrounds with persistence, whether we win or lose, we should still be content with our results. And recognition given to those that stand on a platform has winners, but life honors those that served and fight for what is right.

Wisdom and Knowledge
for All to Seek

With the ancient is wisdom; and in length of
days understanding.

—Job 12:12

Life as given one enough knowledge for one to accept the course of one journey. It has also given you wisdom so one doesn't roam around blindly.

I'm convinced that experience causes one to stand boldly against life and its diverse phase. They say, "No man's position in this life is permanent." Some may define this phrase as "rags to riches." Still, it's also a quote that can claim the prophecy of health, success, beliefs, and direction in one's life. In school, we instructed, informed, directed, and were rewarded for our achievements, but what we prepared for suddenly become unknown because what stood before us was not what was taught.

Halfway through my journey, I've named this phase as "the filler," because as you journey, life fills in its unaware elements that oppose us without preparation. It has shown me its ins and outs but offer no agreement of relief, so there is no refuge from what it provides. I must learn to access observation, which I use to alert me when I am on familiar ground, which I gained from the experiences I have encountered. It has offered me insight so I can be more vigilant in my doings and choices.

I've accepted every battle that life dashes at me because my endurance has boosted my willpower rather than cause me pain. Perhaps I am a weird individual, but no harm is done because I think the same. I try seeing the positivity of my condition rather than the brokenness it should have offered—"a way out" is always a solution to any problem. Still, sometimes we remain in them because they may provide financial security, convenience, or sometimes we would rather not deal with the guilt.

All this can be changeable because what we gain from knowledge is wisdom. This insight will allow you to make choices that will bring restoration, peace, and even value as a person. We see the solution, but as I can tell you firsthand, often I have been lonely, lacking, and confused after these results. So what can you do? I ask. Maybe we should never seek the answers on our own because, as humans, we are not capable of fixing all issues on our own. I believe with all we do, we should seek the intervention of God within all areas of our life.

There you will find the wisdom of which you seek to direct your path. With God's words, we shall find everlasting peace and prosperity. Never think that you will find restoration on your own because "Who is wise and understanding among you? Let them show it by their good life, by deeds done in the humility that comes from wisdom" (James 3:13).

Whether you are a believer or an unbeliever in God, what he is offering is free to all who seek it, as it is said, "Happy is the man that findeth wisdom, and the man that get understanding. For the merchandise of it is better than the merchandise of silver, and the gain thereof than fine gold. She is more precious than rubies: and all the things thou canst desire are not to be compared unto her. Length of days is in her right hand; and in her left-hand riches and honor. Her ways are ways of pleasantness, and all her paths are peace. She is a tree of life to them that lay hold upon her: and happy is every one that retaineth her" (Proverbs 3:13–18).

To say you know what life will offer without knowing what is ahead signifies ignorance, I will say to refrain from bold speeches and presentations because no one has ever traveled the same path twice. "What you sow will determine what we reap." Allow oneself to rise above distracting elements, keep a driving force toward your goals, and suddenly, your obstacles will turn to delusions. Allow yourself to be educated by the experience's life offers, negative or positive; there's wisdom in its midst.

Love and What It's Worth

And above all these things put on charity, which
is bond of perfectness.
                                        —Colossians 3:14

Love—a four-letter word pronounced with simplicity but flowing with influence.

The love of God is the first love that one should experience, followed by the embracing love of one's parents, which allows us to be lovers of oneself; there and then, I believe you can share the love with others.

From my understanding, love is the word that expresses itself through emotion and energy that flows without borders, not by sight. And this brings me to the thought if God is love, then why would I contradict my belief based on not seeing his face? God is love, and his love should be a presence of which brings peace. My testimony throughout this book brings evidence to my experience of the love of God.

One that gives refuge and strengthens in unity, a love of diversity that knows no partiality, a love that brings manifestation which elevates praises and confirms beliefs, a love that flows in abundance, which applied with mercy is a big love given with absence and without obligation.

The self-love I have showered myself with each day as manifested itself because of God's love. The admiration I indulge in is not coming from a place of ego, or pride but a place of contentment and peace. When I look back on where I was coming from and the state of mind I process today, giving thought to all the wrong turns I took, that could have taken me to mental destruction and confusion that would eventually construct my belief today.

I experience my self-love through my purpose because I believe that I can do and have every desire of the heart, based on the knowledge I have gained as a child of God. With the acceptance of who my creator is, I have accepted who I am. But before wisdom, I was lost even though I surrounded by people that love me. I was still struggling to find my place; because of this issue, I grew as a reserved individual.

I never felt the need to desire to change my image. I get conscious about my height, my shortcomings with my ability to pronounce words correctly because it often stands as an obstacle against my courage to stand before an audience or to speak aloud. But I have now freed myself from the personal hindrance I have created within the pathway of my dreams, desires, and purpose. I have now obtained a love that lives within me, through me, and for me, that assures me I am worthy despite my faults.

I can say I am a lover of God, whom I believe created us and all that is within and out of this world, and for me to have a love for God, it stands that I have a passion for my brothers and sisters and all creatures of his creation.

These four definitions of love I offered are the love that created us as humanity, a stronghold of strength and commitment that flows among us as a nation. The love I have for God is a love of oneness. That shows personal appreciation and love to my Creator, for doing his will even for my existence. The trials he allowed as molded me into who I am today, with the assurance of the love he is giving me, it gives me a reason to walk with blinded eyes, knowing that my faith affirmed my path.

God's love, the most mysterious love, offers without condition, with no obligation to return, with no needed requirements. A love that gives protection and one that holds a mass of strength that could move a mountain. One that allows the impossible to be made possible, a love that provides comfort and guarantees assurance. A love that brings forth healing and declares resurrection, a love that redeems continuously without judgment.

Self-love—a love that is unique with no similarity, never to be compared or to be denounced by anyone. A love of acceptance that denies rejections in any form, a love of recognition that affirms one's identity of strength, a love of self-reliance, knowing that freedom is your choice.

Family love—a union that stands on a love of support, loyalty, and forgiveness bonded with an obligation. A love of fellowship that is designed with diversity and a bundle of DNA that affirms oneness.

Humanity love—a love which was created by God's love, a significant addition to this world that displays his love of diverseness. A love that knows no division because we are created to be one. A love of bond with an alliance that brings loyalty, dependence, and refuge. A love of creativity that ensures abundance, one that shows gratitude with fruitfulness, togetherness, and devotion.

Unleash Self-Love to Bind Self-Pity

Fear ye not therefore, ye are of more value than
many sparrows.
                                    —Matthew 10:31

The delusions of elements that stand before me, the conception of my
mental barrenness to overcome my defeat has hindered me from completion. I have known from experiences we were created with authority to be domain over all things, but I've also learned that we also hold
the key to destruction. An element of disaster, brokenness, death, and
failure, but the most potent aspect of damage is of oneself, which we
inflict upon ourselves through ways that express our defeats and fears.

   If I wore every guilt or conviction I bestowed upon myself based
on the action from others and even those I have inherited from my
choices, I could never see and know who I am and what is my purpose in this life. At first, I would blame myself for not being more
vigilant or wiser with my choices, and I would be forced by others to
believe that I was alone on this journey. I realized that just as I carefully placed those negative emotions within my thoughts, I was also
allowing them to be a part of my reality.

   My breakthrough moment appeared when I realized that I was
never alone or abandoned by whatever reason, good or bad; God was
always there. Or you can surrender your purpose by accepting your
defeat without warfare, which instantly places a shackle of limitation,
which defeats your independence.

   You are a product of what you believe in; I trust doing all things
through Christ because I am a creation of his promise, as he bestowed

grace upon my life—restoring me as a new person within his sight and for others to see. By removing any injustice, abuse, hatred, and despair which stand before me and my desires, I genuinely believe that we all can have this peace within ourselves.

Everyone endures burden and stands before barriers; no other can tell of one's endurance or one's sanity. But I can stand and testify that anything that's broken can be fixed. Allow yourself to be your purpose. With boldness, stand before obstacles that lie across your path. With authority, caution it of its temporary causes. This should be driven by your desires to live; this will create a shift along your path of limitation to a way of abundance. These are some of the many obstacles we create within our minds as we selfishly deprive ourselves of greatness.

Self-deception is produced by doubts which reveal the conviction of oneself, the disloyalty we bestow upon our lives, which brings limitations of growth, which is the first step of defeat. The beginning of one's action depends on the mental perspective one chooses for its outcome. In the steadfastness of God's promises, we have the authority to speak freedom, peace, health, and favor over oneself by the mention of his name, Jehovah God.

Self-denial—one should believe that he/she can obtain any desire of the heart. With determination, one should be rewarded for one's endurance. Still, we are the creators of our battles, distraction, and obstacles, within our path to happiness, salvation, success, and prosperity, byways of holding on to past abuse, unforgiveness, and afflictions. One of the most effective elements of self-denial is the spoken words of hate; we allow the wrath of other's opinions to replace growth within our minds as we place disapproval and hostility upon ourselves.

Self-murder—the final element of destruction of oneself, where sinful indulgence has taken place within our lives permanently. We torment our beliefs with the despair of rejection, where bitterness becomes our source of delight and grief replaces joy, as we wear the crown of the unworthy loads of misery upon our heads. And our attire becomes clothed of shame, unforgiving, and regrets, allowing death to receive us gladly.

Only Time Knowingly Unfolds What the Future Holds

He hath made everything beautiful in his time:
also, he hath set the world in their heart, so that
no man can find out the work that God maketh
from the beginning to the end.
—Ecclesiastes 3:11

Time is the master. No one ever defeats time, and no one ever held time; time itself waits on no one. As an achiever, I have always set my goals to achieve each year with time. As my birthday comes around, I've become one year older, and if I hadn't brought my goals to completion, I would break down, crying with disappointment. But this becomes my past because I learned that even though time has passed, it still doesn't mean I should quit.

Time is the essence of your life, and it will flow without ceasing. Our achievements depend on time to manifest itself, but never forget that without the dedication, hard work, and sacrifices, time has nothing to work with. Even the essence of nature, time, has shown authority by changes in its seasons.

Those who attempt to declare life and death upon others without the consent of time and as time proclaims its will, we call it premature death. With the immoral indulgence, many tried to manipulate the sense of time within their lives, utilizing wealth and success. But as time flows, it too will be manifested and tell tales of bad decisions, in which what we sow into this world is what we will reap.

Be careful of evil deeds, immorality, blasphemies, and lies because time will tell its tales; with our beliefs, the time has proven itself by initiating with evidence and understanding, which brings testimony to our beliefs.

Time waits on no one. Time is the order of your purpose, but it will never delay or deny anyone for no reason. What would be your excuse for not fulfilling your mission? Will you say you didn't get enough time? Never think that time will wait on you while you are doubting yourself or your purpose or being persuaded by others that the task is higher than you, being misled by the diversions set by others.

To defeat time is impossible, but to be on time is believable, by accepting that you are worthy of the task, by having the perception that diversions are only illusions created by our enemies and can become affected by our own beliefs. Time will continue to proceed within our life. With our experiences, the rotation of the moon, sun, and stars never show themselves before their time; with such authority, they have never been delayed or deprived or stopped by any obstacles. Time has shown you its power; with its invincibility, it will stand against you and before you and depart from your existence without your authority.

Time heals all wounds. The recovery of one's physical injuries depends on the power of medicine, but the healing of one's wounded heart and mind depends on the strength of time. With forgiveness, one relies on time, because even though one forgave, one may never want to forget. To heal with time, one should forgive and forget. However, memories sometimes used for knowledge also can recreate the past within our present by allowing everyday actions to manifest over the reality, not allowing the essence of time to justify the work or words of others.

If you allow time to heal our wounds, it will bring everlasting happiness within our hearts and mind, and even for those that are among us or those who departed from us. Time creates memories, as a replacement of their existence, which brings laughter, moments, love, and honor to the deceased. An unhealed wound physically or mentally can cause depression, pain, disloyalty, and even disbelief, resulting in a life of burden, regrets, and bad choices. For one to live abundantly, one has to forgive and forget and gives authority to the master of time, who is God, our creator, to heal all wounds without hesitation.

Time will tell all tales. One can never obtain the power to relate his destiny or of others. This all leads back to how driven we are to our purpose, the devotion and endurance one is capable of to succeed. Even the concern of our hearts is only affirmed with time; the promises from others will only be offered with time. The concept of our beliefs, which we illustrate by faith, rely on time for its fulfillment.

One thing I have learned is that no one can never tell a story before time because you only may walk the path of those tales as time orders your steps. Even with religions, we depend on the stories, gospel, and revelation that is written within its time. Hence, others have taken it upon themselves to remove facts from what time has offered to humanity.

With the consideration of creating their own stories ordering the time of judgments, only God, who is the master of time, can bring forth the real revelation of his doing in his own time. Humanity should be careful—what we sow into this world is what given to us. In all we do, the only solution for us to stand comfortably with time is to have patience; if you have invested perseverance with time, there is no doubt that God will reward us in his own time.

A Discern Eye Given with Spirituality

Consider what I say; and the Lord give thee understanding in all things.

—2 Timothy: 2:7

Insight is always mistaken for dreams, imagination, or déjà vu, of one's ability to communicate by spiritual discernment.

The eyes of one soul should be the guardian of one's heart, because the discernment of one's soul is the conscience of alertness and the foresight of either prosperity, happiness, disappointment, and grief. "That the God of our Lord Jesus Christ, the Father of glory, may give unto you the spirit of wisdom and revelation in the knowledge of him" (Ephesians 1:17). Based on experiences, the outcome of some events becomes predictable with everyday actions, and speeches bring you back to a déjà vu moment of insight into what has taken place or what is to come.

I have never allowed myself to rely only on what is displayed before me because every action comes with inner motives. "The eyes of your understanding being enlightened; that ye may know what is the hope of his calling, and what the riches of the glory of his inheritance in the saints" (Ephesians 1:18). You will never completely know another or be able to read within one's intention, either good or bad, until they have reached the stage of accomplishment. I have encounter individuals that display pretense actions before me, just to achieve their wants, giving no thought of what their actions will do to your beliefs.

The heart should give heed to the perception of the soul because it relies on clarity rather than emotions. Always relate to feelings rather than what is displayed before you, because 50 percent of our decisions made from the heart are sometimes misguided decisions. If we would only ask for the intervention of God rather than depending only on our emotions. "And this I pray, that your love may abound yet more and more in knowledge and in all judgment" (Philippians 1:9). This would prevent us from the results of heartbreaks, disappointment, guilt, and bad judgment.

People usually define discernment as spiritual communication, and I will agree—why? Because our soul is the connection to our creator. This connection can come across as a vision, conscience, or a recalled moment of the past, which can be alertness to any decision in our life; I can relate to moments that can be associated with this type of connection. With many of my desires to help others, I have offered ingratitude and sometimes discomfort within my home, which is also my place of sanctuary.

With all these experiences, I could have turned my back against helping others, but instead, with spiritual intervention, I have seen where I could shift my ways of assisting rather than allowing the purpose to come to a halt.

Many believers live without spirituality, and I would not object to your beliefs. Still, from my understanding that God is three divine spirits, which is called the Trinity, the Father, the Son, and the Holy Spirit, "Who's he that overcometh the world, but he that believeth that Jesus is the Son of God? This is he that came by water and blood, even Jesus Christ; not by water only, but by water and blood. And it is the Spirit that beareth witness because the Spirit is truth. For there are three that bear record in heaven, the Father, the word, and the Holy Ghost: and these three are one. And there are three that bear witness in earth, the Spirit, and the water, and the blood: and these three agree in one" (1 John 5:78).

With this understanding, I believe that you can never welcome one and not intercede the others. From my experience, the Holy Spirit is a force of spiritual energy that forms ways of intervening God within your doings. This force acts as guidance to whatever problem you are facing. It also gives direction with your decision, which enables you to have a clear conscience with your thoughts.

I believe that we can never live and communicate within this world without spiritual insight because there will be time, or should I say it is here, where the children of God will only recognize by the Holy Spirit that lives within them. "And I will pray the Father, and he shall give you another Comforter, that he may abide with you forever; Even the Spirit of truth; whom the world cannot receive, because it seeth him not, neither knoweth him: but ye know him; for he dwelleth with you, and shall be in you" (John 14: 16–17). You may be disappointed with the message or the order in which it delivered because it's not the desired message the heart must hear, but being led by discernment is being led by the hands of God.

Walk with Grace, Speak with Authority

⟋⟋

For by grace are ye saved through faith; and that
not of yourselves: it is the gift of God.
—Ephesians 2:8

Even though I was baptized at an early age, I didn't accept God as my savior because I still indulged in sinful pleasures. I have had sex before marriage, bearing children out of wedlock, cursing, etc., just a few of what defines the act of sins. But I could tell you that my circumstances from actions and choices could be far worse or even bring the result of death for me and those around me. But with the experiences, I have learned that we can never serve two masters.

But this grace that God has offered us is not for one individual. So I speak for all, bringing attention to what given from God, even if we, believers or unbelievers, have all received unmerited favor in grace. "To the praise of the glory of grace, wherein he hath made us accepted in the beloved. In whom we have redemption through his blood, the forgiveness of sins, according to the riches of his grace" (Ephesians 1:6–7).

Divine grace—according to Google search, it is a theological term present in many religions. It has been defined as the divine influence which operates in humans to regenerate and sanctify, to inspire virtuous impulses, and to impart strength to endure trials and resist temptation and as individual virtue or excellence of divine origin.

But I will not refer to divine grace on a religious perception because each acquires revelation biblically but interprets it by one's own understanding. So I would rather speak on a righteous concept, in the sense of the quality and moral behavior of humanity. You can only access grace by having faith in God, but from my observation, we all seem as if we have lost hope in our Creator. We forget who we are and who has made us and the worth that God has placed upon us as humans.

Sometimes I ask myself, does humanity even realize that the grace that as granted onto them is unmerited favor? And if recognized, what will be our obligation? The word of God has spoken life over us, but I think that we have deprived ourselves of the spiritual influence of God by being ignorant of the grace that has offered to us. The authority in which we live is through Christ Jesus, who is the beloved son that gives his life for the forgiveness of our sins. "Therefore being justified by faith, we have peace with God through our Lord Jesus Christ: By whom also we have access by faith into this grace wherein we stand and rejoice in hope of the glory of God" (Romans 5:1–2).

But we have taken this authority and created wars against others and among ourselves, accepting evil and desiring sinful pleasures. We also have divided religion with philosophy and theories of doctrines, and this allows the gift of salvation to seen as uncertainty. The prize of divine grace from God is paid with the blood of His son Jesus Christ, who has died on the cross, either you are of a religion, a believer, or an atheist, we all reap the benefit of divine grace.

Even though many of us craved after unrighteousness rather than living life with humility, he still provides his grace upon us. I wonder if God could have the thoughts of man. But if that were so, he wouldn't be the forgiving and merciful God that he is, a God that offers an abundance of love and favor even when others say we are not worthy of his love.

But as humans continue to exist and as we consume our time within the sinful pleasures of the world that distracts our beliefs, with doubts, disbelief, helplessness, and fear within our lives, those blind us from the grace that God has shown us each day. If we let the foul spirit contain our lives, we can never achieve the grace that God has given us, or we will never recognize the unmerited grace that offered to us.

"That in the ages to come he might shew the exceeding riches of his grace in his kindness toward us through Christ Jesus. For by grace are ye saved through faith; and that not of yourselves: it is the gift of God: Not of works, lest any man should boast" (Ephesians 2:7–9).

Allow Life to Break You Gracefully

⚜

The LORD is nigh unto them that are of a broken heart; and saveth such as be of a contrite spirit.

—Psalm 34:18

Anything broken can be restored; the importance of restoration falls with the method of mending and the mentality that used for bonding. I have not fantasized about life being a fairytale because from a tender age, life experiences have reminded me of its reality. I have also heard and knew of others with issues, some of which are sad, and some which bring joy, and others have lost hope, and death has become their escape. Life itself is a beautiful thing, and the experience is a cycle of change that triggers our emotional consciousness.

At times, its result has to do with the choices we made, and at times, we must accept what it offers. I can never tell of another experience. I can never bear one's grief or celebrate one's joy. But I can only speak on my own and from my observations. In the early stages of life, my decision to be rebellious was an act of attention—craving to be heard, but looking back, I wonder if I could speak, what would be my story?

I couldn't have spoken about what I knew little of, and I would have to go through cycles to talk about my experience because it would be of a premature view if I expressed my inner thoughts at such time. Some issues felt as if they were battling with age; only time could unfold what was to come from these moments for its wisdom.

You might think that I would tell you I have lived a life of poverty, but I won't because your state of mind is an exit from poverty.

Your thoughts are a gateway to your ideas, and your beliefs bring forth your reality. Your mindset toward your condition or issues should view ways to achieve positive results or change from the position of which you now stand. But again, this statement could be contradicted because the word *poverty* is defined as "wants and extreme need." But society's only rule is that poverty has been pitiful, by lack of provisions, shelter, and wealth, with no thought that we also can be lacking in love, unity, protection, and acceptance, which we all need to survive this journey of life.

In my home in which I have grown, I have provision and shelter, but the absence of protection and unity was my want. Craving for acceptance from others, I've learned that it will never be achieved because each would offer aid based on his own opinion of you. So I learned to seek acceptance within myself; first, I've learned to accept who I am and the path on which I am journeying on.

All that is happening, good or bad, has had its purpose in molding me into who I am today. Who I am today comes from the effect of being hurt, love, and abused physically and mentally. Being deprived, having the lack, and even being discriminated, but instead of being rebellious as I used to be, fighting back with hate and physically defending myself, I realize that this defense is not only creating isolation. I was also creating a mentality that housed pure vengeance that only ate at my soul.

I'm not saying that one should not defend oneself, but just as you were told to choose your battles carefully, you must also learn the ways of fighting them. During my early age, I was ignorant of all that was going on. Time has offered me healing and even wisdom, and pain has taught me the awareness. Love has given me courage, discrimination has shown me acceptance, and hunger has shown me appreciation. Gradually, as I am allowing God to take control of my life and battles, I can see the pathway of my purpose and the conflicts that will try to render me from it.

I embrace my struggles and love my opponent even more; I also understand that what is yours is yours. And if you ever try to hold on to a position, spouse, friend, or even your beliefs, then you are not content with what's around you, for you, or with you; it means it was not for you. I cannot feel your pain, but I can try to let you see that your needs can be fulfilled. Be like time—it never waits no matter what, and nothing will ever stand in its way.

Power in Your Words, Never Cease to Pray

And whatsoever ye shall ask in my name, that
will I do, that the Father may be glorified in the
Son. If ye shall ask anything in my name, I will
do it.
—John 14:13–14

Your promises are never made to be broken. The value of our existence is shown by the abundance of grace we offer each day of our
lives. With humbleness, we utter our desires, worries, pain, and gratitude in prayers in the presence of your holiness.

I wonder if I am speaking the right words or if it even makes
sense to God. If my request is not given on my time, then and there,
I wonder if he's listening. But as time goes by and my doubts become
testimonies, fear is nowhere to be found, and now I've never ceased
to pray all the time, without shame and apology, because I know
prayers work.

As a nation, we should never cease to pray for protection from
the immorality of this world. Daily, we should cover our fellow
brothers and sisters with the armor of God's words, and we should
all seek guidance from the presence of God not only for our immediate families and friends but for all of humanity. In every season,
we should pray. Whether it's by nature or its life cycles that create
seasons of change in our lives and around us, we should continue to
pray for restoration.

These changes may cause us to see life differently and even
affect our feelings if not grounded. Seasons that bring the devastation

of grief, pain, and battles, this period of change pushes our beliefs in different directions with our emotions, especially in times of death and dismay, allowing us to ask the question why. No human can figure out the ways of gods or his affairs, good or bad. It's all by his will and will always end in his purpose for our life and his glory.

Many may argue that we should never ask God why, but we are mere humans, and just as we can never understand the ways of the Lord, we are not capable of standing before our battles and pain and not show any emotions. Or even with considering thoughts, such as why God allows these happenings to take place, especially when thousands of innocent people die by mass murders, disasters, and even widespread diseases. If anyone could relate to those experiences, they would genuinely have thoughts of why within the time of mourning.

As a person that has experienced God's doing and what he allows, I have come to common grounds with his plan; I still don't understand his doings. Still, one thing I do is learn to accept all things good or bad because I believe that if I were not capable of standing against the afflictions, it would never be in my path. God has placed a foundation on which everyone stands because he already knows that we might make decisions, unwanted sacrifices, accept offers, take chances, etc.

That will bring some effect on our path; we suffer significantly by our actions, but often it's our loved ones and others that hurt, but mostly it's a nation that cries intensely by the choices we make. But the foundation on which we stand can bear the burden of our brothers and sisters; it will wipe away the tears and give a shoulder to lean on in time of rest, open arms in times of comfort and utterance that will bring life and prosperity even during death. Remember that God has no control over our actions because he has given us free will. Still, he will always be there for our needs, not in himself but the structure of humanity.

Humanity should be living by the teachings, beliefs, and actions of God; we are a representation of him. Often, we pray for the declaration of God's doing, but why not be the utterance of God and demonstrate his actions and words of promises among ourselves by speaking words and prayers of protection, love, unity, health, peace, prosperity, and righteousness for humanity?

Even though it may seem that we have lost to the wrongs of others, remember that we are children of God and whatever we touch and speak with the declaration of him shall come to past. Allow the Holy Spirit to dwell within our doing and His presence within our thoughts, actions, and our revelations, allowing humanity to demonstrate humility as we live within his spirit and never lose the courage to continue praying.

I Stretch Forth my Hands with Reverence

Wherefore we receiving a kingdom which cannot be moved, let us have grace, whereby we may serve God acceptably with reverence and godly fear.

—Hebrews 12:28

I could remember I was on a train one morning and an older woman was standing, facing my direction. She offered a pleasant smile, which I much appreciated as I smiled back at her. She immediately started a conversation by asking me if I had children, and I reply, yes.

I told her of their ages and their achievement in school, and she instantly offered compliments of my effort to their accomplishments, which I accepted with a smile. And said, "Thank God also to make it all possible."

To my surprise, her response was not what I expected. "God didn't do anything—it was all you," she replied. Honestly, her response lingers in my mind that day because I was trying to see it from her viewpoint to see if I could relate to what she said.

But I reminisce on the events that happened on my journey of life and experiences, the strangers that offer kind words, those who assisted, the inspiration I received from those that testify on the presence of God. His will, without me extending my hand to ask for help, or even give utterance I am in need, my only doing was to pray secretly, and God openly used others to offer blessings upon my children and me. I wish I could have made her see it from my viewpoint, but the journey was too short for me to comment, and again, I was also amazed by her response.

I would say that humanity should be grateful for its existence, and by doing so, we should show reverence to our creator. With admiration, we should stand before him with an overwhelming heart full of praise, recognizing his manifestation within our lives. Still, our hearts will be the magnet for this power of grace, which stands as our deliverance from bondage, fear, and doubts that invoke us in our times of prosperity, happiness, success, and within our beliefs.

The word count within this book can never represent the number of words I want to use as utterance to express how grateful I am to know that I am a child to the Highest King also our creator. I reflect often where I am coming from and am at peace and assurance of where I am going. Why? Because I've found acceptance, confidence, and harmony with the pathway I journey on, despite all that I have endured through which I felt the urge to ask why. He allowed these afflictions to manifest within my journey, but one thing he has shown is that he will never leave me alone.

In the humility in which humanity should stand before God is with courage and gratefulness but is never bold enough to compare with his powers. Never with fear but honor, understanding that the image of his likeness created us, never to be the same level as its creator. We sculptured by love, so we are of values that should recognize throughout our existence and humaneness that humanity must display in the reverence of equality among each other.

Through righteousness, we must uphold the well-being of our fellow brother and sister, our loved ones, our families, and most of all, God daily within our life. As we give reverence in praise to our creator, we should all offer reverence in gratitude to those that have provided themselves as a tool to make a difference within humanity. And this will allow humanity to rise together again with outstretched hands and hearts fill with glorification to God, placing him back to the forefront of creation and as our creator with reverence.

There Is No Humanity
without God

Having the understanding darkened, being alien-
ated from the life of God through the ignorance
that is in them, because of the blindness of their
heart.

—Ephesians 4:18

I could remember conversing with someone about our beliefs in
God; the argument started when I noticed a tattoo of a symbol on
her arm. I asked what the meaning of her tattoo was. "I am an atheist," she replied. Since I knew nothing about atheism, I was open to
know more about what this movement stood for. I asked if it was a
cult, and she said no. I continued to ask questions why she joined
this organization, what transpired for her to believe in this group.

Her explanation didn't hit any facts for me to consider agreeing
with her option, but I never objected to her belief. I asked if she ever
discovered more about what she was opposed to on a personal level
and if she ever tried to investigate before she drew her conclusion.
She replied no, so I asked if she would know who God is, the role
God has played and still performs within humanity, and on a personal level, if she would try to understand what the spirit of God
offered and what the spirit represented.

After a couple of days, as she returned from her vacation, she
was excited to share a photo of her in a church holding the Bible.
Honestly, I was touched because she had made a step to know more
of what she was told to be against without knowing. And yes, I did
the same on the topic of atheists.

THE HUMAN AND THE DIVINE

Humanity has outgrown the era and belief in God, and so we are abandoning the value of our existence. Science and technology should be appreciated and viewed to the core of showing cleverness, which exercises our ability, which also defines our gifts such as creativity, research, and development, a gifted purpose for being healers and creators to humanity. Instead, they are viewed as a replacement of beliefs and attributes of humanity. Each plays its path respectfully, commanded by the hands of humankind.

An article on the benefit of science from Berkely.edu reads, "The process of science is a way of building knowledge about the universe—constructing new ideas that illuminate the world around us. Those ideas are inherently tentative, but as they cycle through the process of science again and again and are tested and retested in different ways, we become increasingly confident in them."

From my understanding, science is an infective resource to humanity in ways of increasing our knowledge of the life form and nature of which we live. And yes, it is doing what it entitled to do but because of increased dependence and confidence in the analysis and as they apply intelligence to their findings. It has also taken away from our spiritual beliefs, as they try to replace it with experiments of species, as they battle to use evolution to restore the truth of creation, in which they are trying to announce that God is not responsible for our existence.

Technology was achieved with great insight—I admire how our resource of communication equipped with technology, allowing humanity to be connected even with the distance. But this world won't be the same without the disadvantages of the resources that technology and science brings. It has been used to replace physical activity, communication without emotions, reactions, expression, and humaneness amongst humanity. With these facts, many have placed limitations on their beliefs because they cannot perceive the face of God.

"But without faith, it is impossible to please (see) him: for he, that cometh to God must believe that he is and that he is a rewarder of them that diligently seek him" (Hebrews 11:6). It is sad to say, but people only believe in what they can view with the eyes because it's a given prove to facts. I can relate to the understanding, but on one end, it's sad because it refers only to me that humanity only perceives creation and their existence externally and that to me limit the magnitude of their faith.

"But if from thence thou shalt seek the LORD thy God, thou shalt find him, if thou seek him with all thy heart and with all thy soul" (Deuteronomy 4:29).

Humanity is everything with God's love; he's our Alpha and Omega, the beginning and the ending of this world. Even though I believe that with knowledge and free will, humanity might create their judgment. But with the belief in his doing, with the unconditional love he gives, I know he will still show mercy even to those trying to exclude him from humanity. Forgiveness is without boundaries, and love conquers all, and understanding that he is still God and all power is still in his hands assures his love toward humanity.

The Eyes of Diverseness
Still See Purpose

For by him were all things created, that are in
heaven, and that are in earth, visible and invis-
ible, whether they be thrones, or dominions, or
principalities, or powers: all things were created
by him, and for him: And he is before all things,
and by him, all things consist.
                                        —Colossians 1:16–17

Through the eyes of diversity, I see admiration, by the ways of difference I have gained creativity, and with the experiences of diversity, I
still see equality.

Humanity was created with diversity by the hands of God. We
were created in his likeness as a human. He also touches the rest of
creation with the aim of diversity. To know love is to know God,
and by accepting nature, you will understand the differences. I can't
speak on diversification based on a single person's belief because of
the diverse concept of others, which plays through their feelings and
conduct among each other. I am writing with open thoughts on this
quote because it's a needed topic to observe within ourselves and of
others.

The essence of the diversity which brings forth the manifestation of this world with its creation is of no other form but God's
likeness. A likeness which is pleasing to him and should be beneficial
to ourselves and our needs. From my understanding, time and diversity played an influential role within the creation of this world and
humanity. The hands of God have done wonders with diverseness,

forming the levels of the mountains to the lowest of valleys, many combinations that should see with equality.

As an individual, it has played a vital role in our presence, choices, endurance, and beliefs. The love of God in the diverseness of creation, within humanity—every race is significant within its beauty, a miracle by the hands of God. I see the indifference in the human race to look upon his creativity within humanity. In no form should diversity be combined with privilege or used as a weapon of discrimination, and privilege is produced by fear as discrimination is the opinion of ignorance, I would mutter to myself as I observed such acts.

If I should only speak about the cause of the privilege and not talk about those who indulged gladly in the offers made because of fear and selfishness, then I would be seen as a racist toward those of privilege. There are those among humanity that refuse to live, fight, defend, support, or create unity. And some literally live within their needs because of guilt and disbelief of one's worthiness to achieve abundantly, so I would have to say that everyone has his shared responsibility.

Living in a world created with diversity should never bring partiality because it was never meant for such purpose; it should be practiced only within one's self-interest and satisfaction. We should give love and equality to all. I imagine a world of one color or none. Humankind and creatures would be of one nature. I would have to say this world would have to be with no interest because it would be dull and lifeless.

It should be admired with the honor of how great God is, seeing such beauty within humanity, the aroma of fragrance from the trees and flowers of the earth that wrestles with the wind, the method of how night becomes day and how the small trails of rivers created the sea. The miracle of a tiny seed can manifest into a tree that brings forth fruits in every season. Even with life expectancy, beliefs, desires, or purpose, we have seen it brings happiness and despair, good and evil, peace and war, death, and life; all this is diversity.

Just as you can never change the essence of time, you can never change who you are or apologized for your existence; every creation has its distinctiveness. All should greatly appreciate it, but most importantly, by oneself, your difference makes this world so beautiful, and with such beauty, it brings mystical moments that prove God's presence. I would love to see all humans place value upon themselves, individually and more so for others, starting with braking borders of separation with acceptance, giving more thoughts into togetherness by seeing diversity bonded with the hands of equality.

A Single Aim for a Mass Purpose

> For God so loved the world, that he gave his only
> begotten Son, that whosoever believeth in him
> should not perish, but have everlasting life.
> —John 3:16

"What is humanity?"

I will define this from my observation and thoughts. Humanity is the essence of creation, a form of individual that God has touched with his likeness and of his image. "And God said, Let us make man in our image, after our likeness: and let them have dominion over the fish of the sea and over the cattle, and over all the earth, and over every creeping thing that creepeth upon the earth. So God created man in His own image, in the image of God created he him; male and female created he them" (Genesis 1:26–27). Humanity is a variety of humans with races that should combine with equality.

What is their purpose?

The purpose of humanity (my thoughts) is a gift to this world, which God has also created to be used as demigods within his presence, by his will. To stand as a representation of him, to lived and inherent the fullness of his glory. To offer humaneness to yourself and others and to worship him in all that we do. To have dominion over all that he has created and to expand the development of this world, by being creators, teachers, builders, motivators, and leaders. But above all, to demonstrate righteousness within the presence of his spirit, from which we were created.

What is their duty?

Duties are exercised under submission, and submission is to show honor. The mission is in the value we place on our existence and our creator. In all that we do, we should show reverence to God because we are an instrument and are filtered to do his will and speak of his truth. I tried living a life of virtue and show compassion toward my brothers and sisters. I allow myself to offer shelter and to fulfill needs for those that needed. And I have also granted favor in the time of my needs.

"For unto you it is given in the behalf of Christ, not only to believe on Him but also to suffer for His sake" (Philippians 1:29). Never allow the deeds of others to turn your hearts against your fellow humans. Don't give thoughts to the wickedness that others offer. Just be vigilant in all you do and offer forgiveness and give praise to God for his protection and remind yourself that you are for God, not against him. "The steps of a good man are ordered by the LORD: and he delighted in his way" (Psalm 37:23).

What should humanity give?

Based on the knowledge from the Bible, the gratitude God expects from us is to keep his commandment and to give him glory in all our doings. "Make a joyful noise unto the LORD, all ye lands. Serve the LORD with gladness: come before his presence with singing. Know ye that the LORD he is GOD: it is he that hath made us, and not we ourselves; we are his people and the sheep of his pasture. Enter into his gates with thanksgiving, and into his courts with praise be thankful unto him and bless his name. For the LORD is good; his mercy is everlasting, and his truth endured to all generations" (Psalm 100).

These are a few questions I asked myself as I observed the daily activity and experiences of humanity. As an individual, I have had my share of challenges. I have shared them with you because one has to place oneself on the front line if one's aim is for change.

As humanity take back their position and their value as an individual and as a nation. We should create a bond of unity. As human beings, we should stand and endure as a people of oneness, a body that preserves justice and equal rights for all. In ways, guaranteed with fellowship is loyalty that gives evidence of wholeness; in times of despair, we should be able to bring forth peace and renewal of beliefs that God is for us.

Without partiality, we should be able to reinforce our aid of refuge to those which are without protection in any form, to restructure the maintenance of resources that which bring provision to all by applying humaneness within our heart as we live in unity representing one body of Christ. Be merciful as God has been to us, even though we show no mercy toward his doing. No love or belief to our God who still offers his love without judgment, as we indulge in sinful pleasures of evil that cause pain, loss, death, suffering, and destruction for others and within ourselves.

I pray that we all strive for togetherness within our household, communities, and fellowship, never ceasing for a time to pray. Never give up a moment not to be grateful nor to show compassion to our fellow humans; never bring a halt to the ways of enriching our cultures and beliefs that we would hand down to the next generation.

Again, we as humanity must restore our identity because I believe that is a journey on which one should embark as an individual to understand the makings of who God is to us and what one should represent. This will allow one to ask a question and receive answers to what has been lingering within one's heart, to know the value of one's existence, and to understand what is expected of us as human beings. Nothing is wrong, taking a few steps back to seek wisdom and knowledge that could offer us gratitude for the Grace and Mercy God has shown us.

To the youths of this world, I plead to you never to make an excuse because of youthfulness to justified ignorance. Life is about living, and experiences offer wisdom, so why do you live with limitations with one's beliefs and achievements? I commend you on your striving for togetherness because your indifference does not stand in the way of unity and equality, but never forget that you all need the fullness of life activities to inherent what you about to sow. You must know your creator one on one and strive for a personal connection so you can stand and give testimony of His goodness.

Never forget that the honor you show your elders today is a blessing for what you know not of tomorrow. You are never too young to die, so you are never too young to seek the rely on the past to create the future.

Humanity, to know God is to feel God. He is not a God to be seen; he only graces us with his love because we could never contain the fullness of God within our presence. We have a lot to give thanks for even though we have moved on, and some of us challenge his position. He still looks beyond our faults and offers grace and mercy toward us.

Everything has its time and place, and this is the time to rise above your brokenness, failures, abuse, and disbelief. Allow my journey to stand as a guarantee that with perseverance, faith, forgiveness, all with the will and presence of God, which brings restoration, peace, happiness, and wholeness to your life.

For those who have paved the roads of righteousness, continue to be humane to others. To those who have offered themselves as a sacrifice with the honor of being a soldier, speaker, preacher, and leaders, fighting and dying for the truth of which humanity created for, we salute you; your work as not forgotten. We will continue to strive to offer what you have struggled for as an inheritance to generations after generations to come.

My fellow brothers and sisters, the unbelievers and the believers, God is a living God. He is willing and able to do all things, and he is the creator of the world, life, and death, good and bad, but never fail to see the wisdom in his doing. He is still on his throne as the King of Kings, the Lord of Lords, the Highest God, the Roaring Lion of Judah, Jehovah, Lord and Savior for All. And we are still mere humans that still have the privilege to depend upon him and ask for his guidance.

Nothing is wrong for us as humanity to go forward because that is our purpose—to develop, create, supply, and inspire but not without the presence and righteousness of our Creator, who is God.

Poems of Hope and Restoration

Recognition is given to those
which stands on a platform
but life
honors those who stand for truth.

Unity in any form
brings hope,
love,
strength,
and forgiveness,
which create a solid foundation
and equal abundance.

Open my eyes to see with discernment,
construct my mind with mindfulness,
fill my heart with love,
and allow my utterance to be of your power.

There's no good without
evil.
There's no grace without
mercy.
There's no fulness without
void.
There's no life without
death.
There's no existence without
divinity.

To whom that stand before death
with boldness
lived life with an utterance
and authority.

Live life with an abundance
of authority
knowing you are a
child of God.

You're the one that gracefully ceases my burden.
You're the one that affirms
loyalty.
You're the one that excites
my desires
as you mold me
to greatness.

Above all,
one should embrace
his identity
to obtain self-love.

Happiness is purity.
Happiness is innocence.
Happiness is peace.
Happiness is unity.
Happiness is acceptance.

We created by his image,
yet our hearts see with differences.
Creativity bestowed upon us,
yet we chose to destroy.
His grace favored us,
yet we lived without faith.
We granted the will to seek wisdom,
yet we chose ignorance.
His choice is to create us,
yet we chose to be destroyed.

Unveil the eyes
to see with
equality
rather than
diversity.

I wonder if a man would perceive without
Discrimination,
what would his thoughts be?
I wonder if animal instincts enhance intelligence,
wouldn't be the hunter hunted?
I wonder if a man would try living righteously
rather than seem divine,
what would his measures be?
I wonder if our eyes could see beyond motives,
what would we see?
I wonder!
God has made man of his image;
I wonder who God looks like to you?

If love was an island,
its mountains will be the heights of grace that surrounded us.
If love was an island,
its trees would be our refuge and strength.
If love was an island,
its waterfalls would flow over as faithfulness.
If love was an island,
its gentle breeze would delight us, such as the Holy Spirit.
If love was an island,
its soil would be his words on which we stand.
If love was an island? Hmmm, I wonder, what would it look like to you?

Acknowledgment

I want to give glory to God for his presence within my life, my mother, Mrs. Peaches Petgrave, and my loving grandmother Mavis Malcolm, who has encouraged me with words of hope. My son, Andre Cobourine, and daughter, Shi Sewell, who is my pride and joy, the force that keeps me going. To all my families that stood with my kids and me. Special thanks to my second parents, Stanford and Fay Lightbourne, and the rest of the families, and to Dr. Dawn A. Perry and Dr. Philip Burgess, my surgeons, who have gone above and behind to save my life; I sincerely appreciate you. My sister, Alicia Petgrave, for being one of my tools of encouragement to write, and my friend, Natalie L. Davy, for the lovely photo of the cover of this book. Big final thanks to my editor, Paul Dinas, who has helped me create this book. Also, a big thank you to Steve Lane for adding the finishing touches.

About the Author

Terry-Ann Grant offered the testimony of her life as a child and her life as a single parent, to serve as an inspiration to others in times of confusion. She is a massage therapist by day and a writer by night, which is what makes her interesting. She believes that any form of therapy is good for the soul. She was born in Kingston, Jamaica, on February 16, 1976. She now lives and is working toward her purpose as an inspirational author in Queens, New York, with her husband and two kids.

The Human and the Divine offers inspirational quotes and poems of hope and restoration, which give support, resolution, guidance and enable us to see what life experiences can offer, especially with our actions, beliefs, and desires. She has also provided her philosophies of life with definitions and testimonials, which brings them to reality. She believes that battles bring values and often quotes, "There's no limitation to what humanity possesses, but the battle is getting to know our values." And this is where our struggles begin.

As a single parent, her beliefs in allowing the intervention of God within your life will assure your source of guidance, hope, and peace, as He offers all favors of your desires. Her desire for this book is to stand as a tool toward life and the choices we make as an individual and as a nation.

She inspires to share her writing skills on a higher platform to offer inspiration in a testament to others. She also feels this way, she could give back and share her strategy on life and its experiences, with the intention for others to achieve from it. When she is not writing, she likes to enjoy her time spending with her family, traveling, reading, and going dancing. She spends her day off discussing her times shared with her grandmother, who still lives in Jamaica.

To learn more about Terry-Ann, go to https//www.humanitytruth.com or www.linkedin.com/in/terry-ann-grant-68346941.